ADOBE® DREAMWEAVER® CS4
HOW-TOs
100 ESSENTIAL TECHNIQUES

DAVID KARLINS

Adobe

Adobe Dreamweaver CS4 How-Tos
100 Essential Techniques

David Karlins

This Adobe Press book is published by Peachpit.

For information on Adobe Press books, contact:
Peachpit
1249 Eighth Street
Berkeley, CA 94710
510/524-2178
510/524-2221 (fax)

Peachpit is a division of Pearson Education.

For the latest on Adobe Press books, go to : www.adobepress.com

To report errors, please send a note to: errata@peachpit.com

Project Editor: Rebecca Gulick
Copy Editor: Anne Marie Walker
Production Editor: Tracey Croom
Indexer: Rebecca Plunkett
Compositor: ICC MacMillan
Cover and Interior Design: Mimi Heft

ISBN 13: 978-0-321-56289-0
ISBN 10: 0-321-56289-5

9 8 7 6 5 4 3 2 1

Printed and bound in the United States of America

Acknowledgements

Special thanks to the team of editors who made this book come together and vigilantly ensured its accuracy, readability, and fun quotient: Anne Marie Walker; Rebecca Gulick at Peachpit; and technical editor Bruce K. Hopkins. Also my appreciation for the layout work that went above and beyond the call of duty by Tracey Croom and the rest of the Peachpit crew.

Contents

CHAPTER ONE

Creating a Web Site

Many people think of Web design in terms of simply creating a Web *page*. However, before you start designing Web pages, you should define a Dreamweaver CS4 Web *site*. Defining a Web site *before* you create pages allows Dreamweaver to connect your Web pages to each other with links. It makes it possible to embed images or other content (like media) in pages. When you move or rename a Web page (or any file in your site), Dreamweaver updates any links that are affected by that change. And, your Dreamweaver Web site can manage (usually one, but sometimes more) style sheet files that control the formatting of multiple pages across a site.

Defining a Dreamweaver Web site is also necessary when you get ready to transfer your site content from your local computer to a remote server—where others can access your content.

Dreamweaver CS4 has essentially two work environments—the Document window (which has multiple views) and the Files window. The bulk of this book is devoted to using the Document window, and most of your time creating Web sites will be spent in the Document window where you create and edit Web pages. But before you do that, you should be familiar with how Dreamweaver manages Web sites and files in the Files window.

This chapter will help you understand how to manage files in your Web site. In it, you will learn how to define a *remote* Web site and transfer files from your local Web site (your computer) to your remote site, where they will be accessible to everyone over the Internet.

#1 Collecting Site Content

The most basic elements of Web site content are text and images. But the Web is rapidly becoming more accessible and friendly to other types of content: Media files (like Windows Media, QuickTime, or Flash Video), Adobe PDF files, and other types of content are increasingly moving to the "accessible" list. Much of this content requires plug-in software—programs like Adobe Flash Player, Apple QuickTime Player, Microsoft Windows Media Player, Adobe Reader, and other programs that *add* capacity to browsers and are normally installed with browsers.

When choosing content for your site, take accessibility into account. The *most accessible* Web content is HTML text. HTML stands for Hypertext Markup Language—the "hyper" refers not to drinking too many caffeinated beverages but to the fact that Web text includes *links,* clickable text (or images). HTML text downloads quickly and is supported by nearly every viewing device.

Preparing text for Web pages requires bridging the gap between formatting markup language that translates into print formatting (usually PostScript) and formatting markup language that is supported by Web pages. There are several ways to move text to a Web page, but none is completely satisfactory. This is because type formatting in a word processor, like Microsoft Word, has features that are not available in Web formatting, and vice versa.

There are three basic options for bringing type to a Web page:

- Copying relatively unformatted text into Dreamweaver and formatting it in Dreamweaver

- Using export tools in your word processor and import tools in Dreamweaver to translate the markup language from PostScript to HTML

- Saving the text file as an Adobe PDF file, opening the file in a browser using plug-in software, and defining links to the file in a Dreamweaver Web page

There are important advantages to using the first two options. If you copy and paste text from your word processor into Dreamweaver, you can use all the formatting tools provided by Dreamweaver. These tools are designed to apply formatting that can be interpreted well and consistently by browsers. The downside of this method is that you need to reapply formatting in Dreamweaver.

On the other hand, saving your word processing file as an HTML file (some word processors have a Save As Web Page option) allows you to bring as much formatting as possible with the text as you move it into Dreamweaver. The downside of this method is that the formatting generated by your word processor is unlikely to hold up as consistently in browsers as text formatted in Dreamweaver.

Tip

If you're not using Microsoft Word, other word processors like TextEdit, WordPerfect, and OpenOffice all save to Word format. Or, you can copy and paste text from any source (including a Web page that is open in a Web browser) into a Dreamweaver page in the Design window. If you copy and paste, you will lose most or all of your formatting.

If you save a Word file as an HTML page or if you import a Word file into a Dreamweaver Web page, you can clean up the HTML that results by choosing Commands > Clean Up Word HTML. From the Clean Up HTML pop-up menu, choose a version of Word. Then accept the default check box settings. Doing this will strip from the generated HTML any coding that would confuse browsers (**Figure 1**).

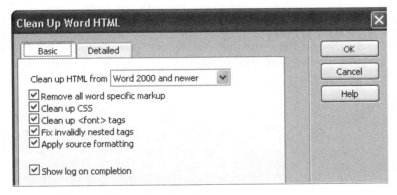

Figure 1 Cleaning up imported HTML code.

Many programs (Adobe Photoshop and Photoshop Elements among the most prominent) allow you to export image files to JPEG, GIF, or PNG format. These programs provide you with advice on when to use which format. Here, I'll list a few basic attributes of the various formats:

- **JPEG** images support millions of colors and are best for photographs. *Progressive* JPEG files "fade in" as they download rather than appearing line by line.

(continued on next page)

Importing Spreadsheets and Word Documents in Dreamweaver CS4 for Windows

The Windows version of Dreamweaver allows you to import Microsoft Word (and Excel) files directly to Web pages. This saves the step of opening the file in a word processor and saving it as an HTML file. To import a Word or Excel file, open the Web page to which you are importing the file, and choose File > Import > Word Document (or Excel Document). The Import Document dialog opens, and you can choose a few options for importing, ranging from Text Only (no formatting) to Text with Structure Plus Full Formatting (which retains the most formatting).

Differences Between Print and Web Images

Preparing images for the Web presents a separate set of challenges than preparing images for print. There are several major differences between images on the Web and images prepared for print documents. These differences include these parameters:

- Web images are usually saved at 72 dots per inch (dpi), whereas print images are routinely saved at 300 dpi and higher resolution.

- Web images are saved using the RGB (Red, Green, Blue) color system, whereas print images usually use CMYK (Cyan, Magenta, Yellow, Black) color mode.

- Web images are saved to JPEG, GIF, or PNG format, whereas print images are often saved in the TIFF format.

- **GIF** images support far fewer colors than the JPEG format and are not usually used for photos. But GIF images support *transparency*, which allows the background of a Web page to show through empty spots in the image. GIF images can be defined as *interlaced*. Interlacing, like the progressive attribute in JPEG images, allows the image to fade in as it downloads.

- **PNG** images support more colors, like JPEG, and allow you to define a transparent color, like GIF files. However, PNG format is generally not acceptable for photos because it lacks the JPEG format's capacity to manage colors and photo detail.

Programs like Photoshop allow you to preview how images will look in all three formats with different quality settings. High quality preserves color and image quality. But high-quality images (and large ones) take longer to download than small or low-quality images.

Programs like Adobe Illustrator, Photoshop, and Photoshop Elements have Save for Web features that can assist you in preparing images for the Web.

Images that have a small file size and fast downloading time (and generally therefore low-quality) are generated using *compression*. Compression "looks for" pixels in an image that do not need to be saved as part of the file information, and it reduces file size by saving less of the image definition.

#2 Defining a Local Site

Dreamweaver manages all your file connection issues, as long as you *start by defining a Dreamweaver Web site.* This Web site manages your files for you. If you change a filename, Dreamweaver updates the links throughout your site. If you go on an organizing binge and decide to move all your images into appropriate file folders, Dreamweaver updates the links throughout your Web site. Again, just to emphasize, this works as long as you 1) set up a Dreamweaver Web site, and 2) do *all* your file management (renaming or moving files) in the Dreamweaver Site panel.

Now that I've stressed the importance of creating a local site, here's how you do it:

1. Collect your entire site content in a single folder. You can create subfolders (subdirectories) for images, media, Web pages, and so on. But all these folders must be within the folder that will serve as your local site folder.

2. From the Document window menu, choose Site > New Site. The Site Definition dialog opens.

3. At the top of the dialog, click the Advanced tab to see all the options at once instead of a wizard that reveals only one element of the site at a time. In the Category list, choose Local Info (**Figure 2**).

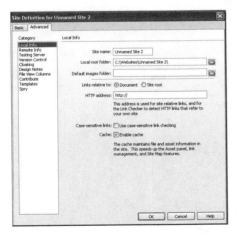

Figure 2 Defining a local site.

(continued on next page)

But I'm a Designer

"I'm a designer, not a file manager!" I hear you. File management is not my favorite part of Web design either. Web sites, especially the latest generation of Web sites, involve a *lot* of files. In addition to the HTML file that stores your basic content, Web pages often involve image files, media files, JavaScript files to control animation and interactivity, CSS (style sheet) files to control formatting, and more! Fortunately, Dreamweaver handles all the work of ensuring that these files are linked properly, work together, and can be easily transferred from your local computer to a remote server.

4. In the Site name box, enter any text you want. Nobody will see this text but you and other developers: It is simply descriptive information to help you remember which Web site this is.

5. In the Local root folder area, click the folder icon at the right and navigate to the folder in which you saved all your files. Or, if you have not collected any files yet, create a new folder and designate that as your local root folder.

6. If you want Dreamweaver to automatically save images to one folder on your local storage system (usually a hard drive), you can navigate to a folder using the folder icon next to the Default images folder field. This is not a particularly essential option, and it can get in your way if you want to manually control where your files are stored.

7. Choose the Links relative to Document option. This is the most efficient and reliable way to generate and update links between files, and to define links for embedded images.

8. The only other important option is the Enable cache check box. This activates the Asset panel that displays all site content.

9. With your local site defined, click OK. Dreamweaver is now ready to organize your files for you.

#3 Organizing a Local Site

When it's time for housekeeping and moving files from one folder to another, you can also rely on the Dreamweaver Files panel. You can display the Files panel by choosing Window > Files or by pressing the F8 function key (Windows) or Shift+Command+F (Mac) to toggle between displaying and hiding the Files panel (**Figure 3a**).

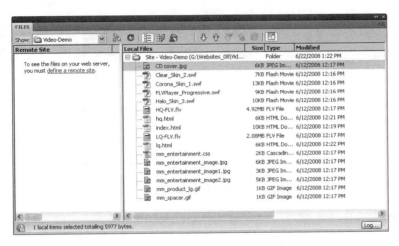

Figure 3a Viewing the files in your Web site in the Files panel.

The Files panel menu has options for typical file management actions, like creating new files or folders, renaming files, copying or pasting files, deleting files, and so on.

The basic rule for working with files is this: *Never* change filenames or move files between folders using your operating system's file management tools. Instead, *always* rely on Dreamweaver's Files panel to manage filenames and to move files between folders.

The Site folder looks and works like the Finder (for Mac) and Windows Explorer (for Windows) utilities. It allows you to drag files between folders, copy and paste files, rename files, and delete files, just as you would do in Finder or Explorer.

Why should you use Dreamweaver's Files panel? Because in a Web site, files are almost always connected to other files. You might have an image embedded in a page. If you change the name of that image file or move it to another folder, the link between that image and the page in which it is embedded becomes corrupted.

8

8

Index.htm or Index.html Is Your Home Page

Different servers have different rules for home pages, but generally the index.htm or index.html file serves as a Web site home page. The home page is the file that opens when a visitor comes to your site. This has more significance when your site is transferred to a remote server and made accessible to visitors. But even when you are only working with a local site, defining a home page is necessary to generate a site map or prototype navigation links using the Dreamweaver Files panel.

However, if you do all your file management in Dreamweaver, Dreamweaver will *fix* the problems caused by moving or renaming a file by redefining links that involve that file. For instance, if files in your Web site contain links to a file and that filename is changed, Dreamweaver will prompt you to change those links in an Update Files dialog (**Figure 3b**).

Figure 3b Dreamweaver redefines links to match a changed filename.

When you define your local Web site in Dreamweaver, you define a local site folder. Dreamweaver knows that this folder is where all your site files *should be* kept. If you open a file from another folder or copy or move a file from another folder, Dreamweaver will prompt you to save a copy of that file in your Web folder. For example, if you embed an image in a Web page, Dreamweaver will prompt you to save that image to your site root or image folder when you place it on the page.

#4 Managing Sites

Dreamweaver CS4's Files window provides three ways to look at your site. The default view is the Site Files view. For all practical purposes, this is the view you will work in. It allows you to see your Files window as a split screen with your local site (the files on your computer or local server) on the right and your remote site on the left. Until you define a remote site (see #5, "Defining a Remote Site"), you won't see any files at the remote server. But as soon as you define a local site, you can see a list of all the files at your local site.

Two other views are in the File window: The Testing Server view is for data-driven Web sites, where data from a database at a remote server is embedded in Web pages. That advanced approach to building Web sites relies on extensive server scripting and database programming, and is beyond the scope of this book. The third view is the Repository Files view for people using Adobe's Subversion technology to coordinate large sites with multiple remote developers.

Other important tools in the Files window are the Connect icon, which connects the Files window to your remote site; the Refresh icon, which refreshes local and remote site views; and the Collapse/Expand icon, which toggles between a small, collapsed Files window and an expanded Files window. There are more icons in the Files window that manage file transfer between remote and local sites. These are explained in #6, "Uploading To a Remote Site" (**Figure 4a**).

Duplicate, Export, and Import

The Export and Import options in the Manage Sites dialog do not, as you might readily assume, export or import *Web sites*. Instead, they export and import *Web site settings*. These settings are valuable because they define things like login information and paths where files are stored. But again, they cannot be used to back up an entire Web site. To do that, use the Copy option. Duplicating a Web site creates a backup of that site.

Figure 4a Icons in the expanded Files window.

In addition to creating new sites, you can edit site properties, duplicate a site (to create a copy of that site), remove a Web site from your computer, or export and import sites using the Manage Sites dialog.

To access the Manage Sites dialog, choose Site > Manage Sites. If you have multiple Web sites on your computer, choose the site you want to edit from the list on the left side of the dialog (**Figure 4b**).

Figure 4b Selecting a site to edit.

Note
You might be managing many Web sites from a single computer. A professional Web designer, for example, will likely work on the sites of many clients from his or her computer.

With a site selected, choose from the set of options on the right side of the dialog.

Use the Edit option to reopen the Site Definition dialog. Here you can revise any of the information that defines the local or remote sites. So, for example, if you change your remote Web host provider, you can enter new Web host information this way.

The Duplicate option is sometimes useful in creating an experimental site. Or, if you are using one site as a "template" to create other sites, you can copy the original site, and then edit the definition of the new site and make changes to customize it.

The Export feature in the Manage Sites dialog allows you to save site settings as a distinct STE file. This file can then be used to restore the site settings on another computer.

You can export your site settings as an XML file that you can import into Dreamweaver later. This enables you to move sites between machines and product versions or to share settings with other users.

To export site settings, follow these steps:

1. Select Site > Manage Sites, and then select a site from the list on the left side of the Manage Sites dialog. With the site selected, click the Export button on the right side of the dialog. The Exporting Site dialog opens.

2. If your site contains a login name and password for your remote server, a dialog will appear with the option of letting you back up your site settings, including user name and password as well as local path information. To back up your site with this information included, choose the first option. To back up site settings *without* user name and password so you can give the password to other users, select the second option (**Figure 4c**).

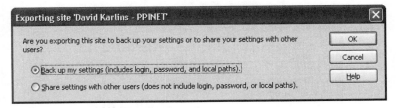

Figure 4c Backing up site information, including user name and password.

3. Click OK, and then click Done in the Manage Sites dialog.

When you back up site information, you create an XML file to which Dreamweaver CS4 attaches an .ste filename extension. This file can be opened using the Import feature in the Manage Sites dialog to install Web site settings for a site that has already been exported.

Local vs. Remote Sites

Normally, there are two versions of your Web site. The local site, on your computer, is where you create content. When that content is ready for the public, you upload it to the remote server.

In order for the remote (publicly accessible) site to match the content on your local site, all files must be transferred correctly, maintaining the same filenames and folder structure as exists on the local site. Dreamweaver provides the Files panel to manage your local site content, and you use the same Files panel to manage your *remote* site.

#5 Defining a Remote Site

Normally, a remote server presents content developed on a local site. In other words, most developers first create and test their Web pages on their own computer and then upload that content to a remote server once it has been tested, proofread, vetted and approved, and deemed ready to share.

If you do not yet have a remote site, there are many vendors ready to sell you one. When you obtain a remote server, make sure the provider gives you the following information:

- The FTP location

- Your login name

- Your password

Some sites require more login information, but you will definitely need the three items listed (**Figure 5a**).

Dear davidkarlins,

Welcome to AtFreeWeb.com. Below is your new account information. Please read carefully before logging and publishing to your site.

User Name:	activeip\david
Password:	000000
FTP server:	ftp.atfreeweb.com
Home Directory:	david
Web Root Directory:	david

Figure 5a Login information supplied by a Web server provider.

With this information, you'll be able to tell Dreamweaver how to access your remote server, and Dreamweaver will handle all the technical details of making a connection and transferring files.

When you launch Dreamweaver, the site you had open at the end of your last session will open. Your open site is indicated in the Files panel (**Figure 5b**).

Signing Up for a Remote Server

Shopping for a Web host can be simple if you are creating a small site with small files and not expecting a lot of traffic. Yahoo!, for instance, offers a deal for about five dollars a month, and often throws in a free domain name (the name people type in their Web browser to get to your site— like davidkarlins.com).

If you plan to include large files (like video) or expect a lot of visitors (over 100 a day), or both, do some comparison shopping before choosing a Web host. The site www.buildyourown website.us has useful resources and articles for finding Web hosting and obtaining domain names.

Creating a Web Site

Selected site in Files panel

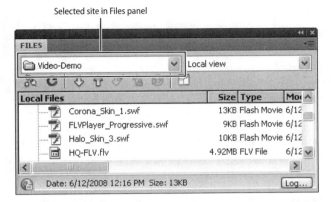

Figure 5b Identifying the open site in the Files panel in collapsed view.

To define a remote connection, choose Remote view from the View pop-up menu in the Files panel menu bar (**Figure 5c**).

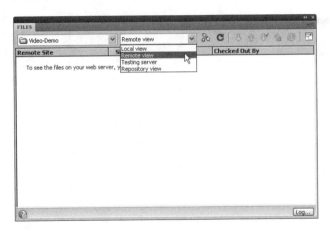

Figure 5c Choosing Remote view.

When you select Remote view, if you have not defined a remote server yet, the Files panel displays a link to define a remote site (**Figure 5d**).

To see the files on your web server, you must define a remote site.

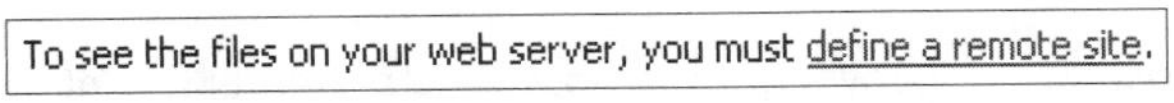

Figure 5d Open the Site Definition dialog to define a remote server connection.

Click the link to open the Site Definition dialog with the Remote Info panel selected. In the Site Definition dialog, choose the Advanced tab.

Tip

Both the Basic and Advanced tabs provide access to the tools necessary to define a remote server connection, but the Basic tab marches you through multiple wizard-type screens, whereas the Advanced tab provides easier access to an overview of your connection options.

In the Advanced tab of the Site Definition dialog, click the Remote Info category. Then follow these steps to define your remote server:

1. From the Access drop-down menu, choose FTP to define a connection to a remote server, or choose Local/Network if the remote site will be on another computer on your internal network (**Figure 5e**).

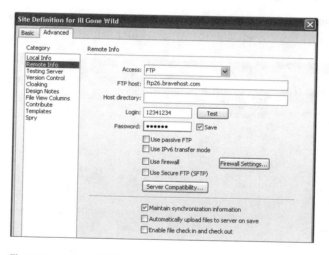

Figure 5e Defining FTP location, login, and password.

2. In the FTP host field, enter the FTP location provided by your Web host provider.

3. In the Host directory field, enter the server folder information provided by your Web hosting company, if needed.

4. If your Web hosting company requires a host directory, enter the information the hosting company provided in the Host directory field.

5. In the Login field, enter the login or user name provided by your Web host provider.

6. In the Password field, enter the password provided by your Web host provider.

   Note
   Password and login information is case sensitive and must be entered exactly as provided. Once you have entered an FTP location, a login, and a password, you have defined the essentials of your connection.

7. If your Web host provider allows you to connect using passive FTP, select the Use passive FTP check box. You can try connecting to your site without this check box selected, and then try enabling passive FTP if your connection fails.

8. If you are working behind a firewall, your system administrator might need to configure the firewall settings in the Site Definition dialog. However, normally Dreamweaver adopts the same firewall settings you use with other programs to connect to the Internet, so custom settings are not necessary.

9. After you define the remote connection, click the Test button. If your connection works, the confirmation dialog appears (**Figure 5f**).

   Note
   For now, ignore the three check boxes at the bottom of the dialog that define synchronized, automatic, and shared file management options. The check-in feature is for large sites with multiple developers.

Figure 5f A successful server connection test.

#6 Uploading To a Remote Site

Simply defining a remote server connection does not automatically *connect* you to that server. When you open a Web site in Dreamweaver, you normally open only the local site. It is only after you actually *connect* to your remote site that you can see the files on that site and manage files at the remote server.

With a site open, you connect to your remote server by clicking the Connects to remote host icon in the Files panel (in either Expanded or Collapsed view). Once you connect to a remote server, you can see either local or remote server content using the View pop-up menu in the Files panel. To see the content of both the local and remote sites at the same time, click the Expand icon in the Files panel toolbar. In Expanded mode, click the Site Files icon in the Files panel toolbar (**Figure 6a**).

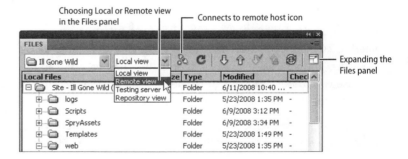

Figure 6a Connecting to a remote server via the Files panel.

Getting comfortable with transferring files in all three environments (Document window, expanded Files panel, and collapsed Files panel) allows you to conveniently and quickly transfer files and easily keep track of what is where.

There are two basic phases to transferring files to a remote server. The first phase is when you design the original site on your local computer, and then upload the whole site to your remote server. The second phase is when you edit elements of your site—first making changes to the local version, and then uploading only the changed parts of your site to the remote server.

Although you can edit Web pages while files transfer to (or from) a remote server, you cannot do other file management activities on the server while files are in transit. This means, for example, that you cannot

Transferring Files in the Document Window

In Chapter 2, you'll explore the Document window in detail (see #7, "Exploring the Document Window). However, it is helpful here to note that you can transfer files from the local site to the remote site, or vice versa, in the expanded Files panel. You can *upload* files to the remote site directly in the Document window. And you can view the local and remote sites in the collapsed Files panel.

edit your site in the Site Definition dialog while you are transferring files. But you can open a Web page on your local site and edit it.

To upload an entire site from your local folder to the remote server, click the root folder of your local site in the Files panel—either in Expanded or Collapsed view. With the root folder selected, click the Put File(s) icon in the Files panel toolbar (**Figure 6b**).

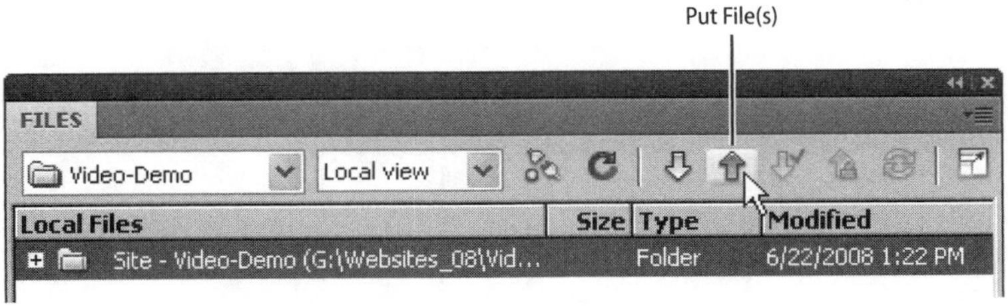

Figure 6b Uploading an entire Web site.

Dreamweaver will prompt you to confirm the action by clicking OK, and then it will upload your entire Web site. The Background File Activity dialog will track the progress of uploading your site (**Figure 6c**).

Figure 6c Transferring files in the background—you can continue editing pages in Dreamweaver while files transfer.

Once you have uploaded your site, you won't want to waste time re-uploading the entire site each time you change a file. Instead, you can upload selected files. Shift-click or Ctrl-click/Command-click to select files in the Files panel, and choose Put to upload the selected files.

Coordinating Local and Remote Sites

As a general rule, avoid editing filenames, folder locations, and so on at your remote server. If you stick to a protocol of creating and managing files on your local site, and then transferring those files to the remote site, you'll ensure that both sites match—what you see on your local site will match what visitors see at your remote site.

The Dreamweaver Files panel provides tools for managing files at both the local *and* remote servers. That is a potentially scary power to have. It means that you can rename, move, and delete files from your remote server and, in the process, corrupt your remote server files so they no longer match the files on your local server. This is part of the reason why standard procedure is to edit files on a local site before uploading to a server.

You can also upload open pages directly from the Document window. Do this by clicking the File Management tool in the Document toolbar and choosing Put (**Figure 6d**).

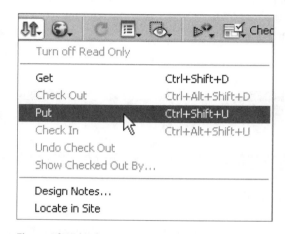

Figure 6d Uploading an open Web page.

In addition to putting (uploading) files to your server, you can also download files from your server. If you are the only person working on a Web site (the only person who places files on the server in Dreamweaver), you will rarely need to transfer files from the remote server to your local computer. Because all files originate on your local computer, you can overwrite files on the server by uploading the matching file from your local computer. However, if you are working with other developers on a site, you might need to download a file that was updated by someone else. In that case, click the file in the server, and then click the Get File(s) icon in the Files panel toolbar (**Figure 6e**).

Get File(s)

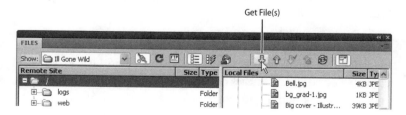

Figure 6e Downloading a file using the Get File(s) icon in the Files panel.

You can synchronize either files you have selected (by Shift-clicking) in the Files window, or your entire site. And you can synchronize your site either by updating the server with newer files from the currently open local site, or vice versa (moving newer files from the server to your local computer).

To synchronize your local and remote sites, follow these steps:

1. From the main Dreamweaver menu, choose Site > Synchronize Sitewide. The Synchronize Files dialog appears.

2. From the Synchronize pop-up menu in the Synchronize Files dialog, choose either selected files or the whole site.

3. In the Direction pop-up menu, choose from the options—get from server, put to server, or both—that allow you to transfer files from local site to server, server to local site, or both ways, replacing older files with more recent ones (**Figure 6f**).

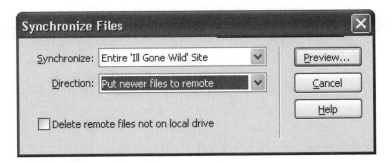

Figure 6f Synchronizing files for an entire site; moving newer files to the remote site.

4. In the Synchronize Files dialog, click the Preview button. Dreamweaver connects to your remote site and creates a list of files that meet your criteria (new at the remote site, newer at the local site, or both). The list is displayed in a dialog (again) called Synchronize. Click OK, and Dreamweaver will update all files according to the criteria you defined.

Dependent Files

If you transfer a Web page with an embedded image to a remote server, a dialog opens asking if you want to also upload *dependent files*. These are files that open along with the page. An embedded image, for example, appears when a page is opened in a browser. The page won't work correctly without the photo being uploaded to the server along with the page. Therefore, you need to include dependent files if you are uploading a page with an image. The next time you upload that page, however, you do not need to re-upload the image file unless you have changed it.

Other files that Dreamweaver considers dependent are style sheets that define how a page looks. Embedded media files are also considered dependent files.

What is *not* considered a dependent file is any page or other file to which that page is *linked*. For instance, if you upload a page that links to another page, you *still need to manually upload* the page to which the uploaded page is linked (if the linked page is missing or has been changed).

CHAPTER TWO

Creating Web Pages

In Chapter 1, "Creating a Web Site," I emphasized the importance of *starting* out by creating a Web *site* in Dreamweaver. If you've done that, you're ready to start designing Web pages in Dreamweaver's Document window.

The Document window is the basic workspace in Dreamweaver. The Document window is where you design Web pages. In the Document window, you can open many pages at a time and edit them. You use the Document window to create or paste text, embed images, define links, place and sometimes create page elements like style sheets (that control the look of a page), input forms, embed animation, and create interactive objects (that react to actions by a visitor).

With Dreamweaver CS4's new Live view, you can also *test* pages in the Document window, checking links, viewing media files, and interacting with the page as if you were in a browser.

In addition to the option of creating Web pages from scratch, Dreamweaver CS4 offers many options for using professionally designed pages as templates and editing them. In this chapter, you'll explore the process for creating your own pages and how to adapt Dreamweaver's extensive set of samples and templates.

#7 Exploring the Document Window

You work in the Document window when you open an existing Web page or when you create a new one. Use the File menu to open an existing Web page (File > Open or File > Open Recent to access a list of recently opened pages) or to create a new Web page (File > New).

When you choose File > New, the New Document dialog opens. Throughout this book you will explore some of the more useful categories of new documents, but the first and main type of new document you'll create in the New Document dialog is a basic page. The basic and main type of Web page you'll create is an HTML page (**Figure 7a**).

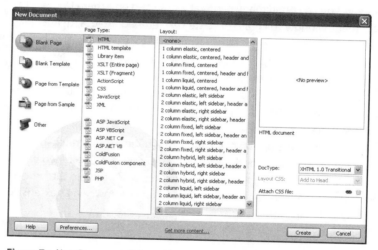

Figure 7a New Document dialog with a new HTML Web page selected.

Clicking the Create button in the New Document dialog generates a new page and opens that page in the Document window. The Document window is crammed with features. The objects floating around in the Document window are mainly panels, menus, and toolbars, which you'll explore in the following how-tos in this chapter. But there are plenty of useful (and sometimes unintuitive) features in just the Document window that should be part of your design arsenal.

The Document window can display with three views: Code, Design, and Split. Code view displays *only* code and is used by designers who want to bypass Dreamweaver's ability to generate code. Design view hides most code, providing a graphical design interface. Split view displays code on the top of the Document window and a graphical design environment on the bottom (**Figure 7b**).

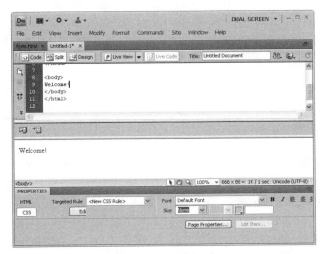

Figure 7b Split view in the Document window displays code on top and a graphical design interface on the bottom.

There are a number of advantages to working in Split view, both for designers who know how to write code, as well as for designers who are not comfortable or proficient in writing their own code. Split view is a way for proficient coders to see a graphical representation of the code they are writing. And Split view is a good way for designers who are not conversant in coding to become familiar with coding, since generated code appears as you create elements in the graphical design window. Even though Dreamweaver is the best existing program for generating HTML and other page layout code, there are times when the only way to troubleshoot a design problem is to edit the code directly. If you edit code in Split view, you can see the effect by clicking in the lower (graphical) window.

Stripped of menus and panels, the main features available in the Document window are rulers, the tag selector, and the status bar. Horizontal and vertical rulers provide a quick way to judge the size of your page and objects on it. Hide or change ruler attributes by choosing View > Rulers. The Rulers submenu lets you show or hide rulers and change the unit of measurement from the default pixels to centimeters or inches.

More Ways to Split Views

You can split your screen vertically instead of horizontally to show code on the right side and the Design view on the left. Or, you can switch and display code on the left and the Design view on the right. To manage how views are split, choose View > Split Vertically. When you do this, a new menu option becomes active in the View menu that allows you to switch the left and right sides of the display.

The tag selector on the left side of the status bar on the bottom of the Document window allows you to select specific tags for editing in the Property inspector (the Property inspector is discussed in #8, "Managing Panels"). The tag selector is especially handy when you're working with objects like tables or embedded CSS (page design objects) and simply clicking an object in the Document window can be difficult (**Figure 7c**).

```
<body> <h3>
```

Figure 7c The body tag in the tag selector section of the status bar.

The right side of the status bar has some handy tools that aid in design techniques.

- The Select and Hand tools provide two ways to navigate around your document. The Select tool is the default mode; it allows you to click on objects or click and drag to select text. The Hand tool works like similar tools in Adobe Photoshop or Illustrator, allowing you to grab a section of the page and drag it in or out of view.

Note
In Split view, the Select and Hand tools are only active when working in Design view, not Code view.

- The Zoom tool is used to draw a marquee and enlarge a section of a page.

- To exit either the Zoom or Hand tool mode and return to the default cursor, click the Select tool.

- The Set Magnification drop-down menu is another way to define magnification.

- The Window size display indicates the size of your Design window, normally in pixels.

- The File Size/Download Time display estimates download time for the page parameters (**Figure 7d**).

Select tool — Zoom tool — Window size

Hand tool — Set Magnification drop-down menu — File Size/Download Time display

Figure 7d Tools in the status bar.

You can adjust the units displayed for window size or the connection speed used to estimate download time in the Status Bar category in the Preferences dialog. On the Mac, choose Dreamweaver > Preferences and in Windows choose Edit > Preferences, and then select the Status Bar category to edit these parameters.

Many of Dreamweaver's page design tools are most easily accessed through toolbars. The Standard toolbar has some basic tools that are common to almost any application. The Document toolbar, on the other hand, provides access to an underappreciated set of rather powerful page design and management tools. The toolbars reside at the top of the Document window and are displayed (if they are hidden) by choosing View > Toolbars.

The tools in the Standard toolbar allow you to create new files, open existing files, print code, copy, cut, paste, and undo or redo an action. All these features are accessible from either the File or Edit menus (**Figure 7e**).

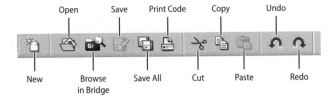

Open   Save   Print Code   Copy   Undo

New   Browse in Bridge   Save All   Cut   Paste   Redo

Figure 7e The Standard toolbar.

The Document toolbar contains some of the most frequently used tools for page design and management. The three buttons on the left allow you to toggle between Code, Split, and Design views.

The Document toolbar also provides a convenient way to define a page *title*—the page "name" that displays in the title bar of a visitor's browser. You define a page title by typing the text to be displayed in the Title box in the Document toolbar.

Using the Code Inspector

Dreamweaver's Code Inspector window—available in both Windows and Mac versions—is accessed from the Window menu (Window > Code Inspector). The Code Inspector is a highly functional code-writing environment and is different than Code view in that it functions as a panel that can be used in Design view. The Code Inspector includes a toolbar that provides prompts as you enter code, as well as prepackaged code snippets. The Code Inspector allows you to collapse or expand sections of coding, making it easier to focus on and edit sections of code.

The rest of the Document toolbar tools are used for managing documents, document display, and file management (**Figure 7f**).

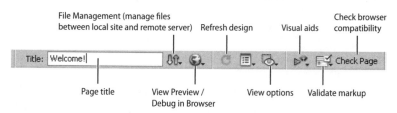

Figure 7f Entering a page title in the Document window.

The browser-compatibility check icon allows you to choose from a variety of Web standards, and then choose actions (validating the open document, selected files, or all the files in your site). Choose Settings from the pop-up menu associated with this icon to define the browsers and versions of browsers that your page will be tested for compatibility with (**Figure 7g**).

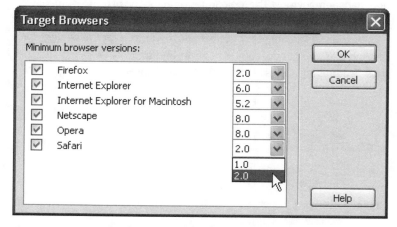

Figure 7g Choosing browsers and browser versions that Dreamweaver will use as HTML standards to test your page for compatibility with.

The Preview / Debug in Browser tool allows you to see how your page will look in a browser window. View options include displaying (or hiding) rulers, guides, and grids. Visual aids include displaying borders of tables, frames, and CSS objects—borders that are not displayed in browsers but are handy for design purposes.

#8 Managing Panels

Many of the features explored in other chapters and how-tos in this book are available in *panels*—rectangular boxes that are normally aligned to the right of the Document window. While each panel obviously controls different features of your Web site or Web pages, panels have some common features (**Figure 8a**).

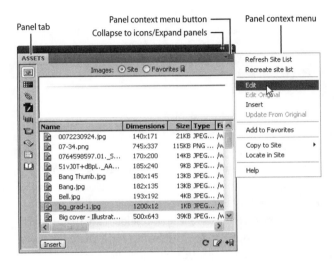

Figure 8a Elements of Dreamweaver panels.

You display panels by selecting them from the Window menu. Active panels display with check marks next to them in the Window menu.

You can relocate panels from their default position on the right side of the Document window by dragging on the title bar.

You can combine or separate tabbed panels by dragging the title bar of the ungrouped panel or by dragging the tab of a grouped panel (**Figure 8b**).

Other Uses of the Property Inspector

You will likely use the Property inspector mainly to apply attributes to text and images. But the Property inspector also adapts to and provides formatting options for other selected page elements.

If you select a table, you can define table size, number of columns, number of rows, cell padding (space between cell content and the edge of a cell), cell spacing (space between cells), table background color, and other attributes. If you select a table *cell,* you can define horizontal and vertical alignment, cell width and height, cell background color, and other alignment and color attributes.

Input forms and their embedded form fields have attributes that can be edited in the Property inspector as well.

More complex page design elements like AP div elements or div tags also have definable attributes that can be edited in the Property inspector.

Figure 8b Adding a panel to a tabbed group.

The Properties panel—usually called the Property inspector—is a unique and special type of panel. It is adaptive in that it allows you to edit properties of a selected object and is somewhat similar to the Object bar in many Adobe applications. For example, if you select text, the Property inspector makes available options for formatting type, including type size, type font, type style, and link attributes (**Figure 8c**).

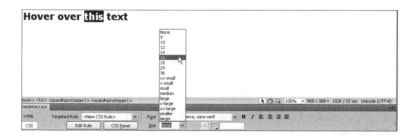

Figure 8c With text selected, the Property inspector allows you to define type attributes.

Or, if you select an image, the Property inspector makes available image-formatting attributes, like image size, ALT text (alternate text to make your image accessible to visitors or browsers unable to view images), or hotspots (clickable linked areas within an image).

#9 Using the Insert Toolbar

The Insert toolbar, also referred to as the Insert bar for short, is the ubiquitous blue-collar power tool of Dreamweaver. Because this toolbar provides access to the bulk of Dreamweaver's features, many developers keep it displayed at all times for quick access to features that can also be found, less conveniently, in menu options or panels. A large percentage of Dreamweaver features, ranging from everyday (inserting images) to esoteric (detailed database management), are accessible from the seven basic tabs in the Insert toolbar. There is also an eighth, customizable Favorites tab. You will be introduced to features accessed through the Insert toolbar throughout this book. Here, the point is to get comfortable with how the Insert toolbar works.

The Insert toolbar is a *set* of toolbars. You get the whole package: Common, Layout, Forms, Data, Spry, InContext Editing, Text, and Favorites.

To display the Insert toolbar, choose View > Toolbars > Insert. You can drag the Insert toolbar to the top of the Document window, or it can float like any other panel. By default, the Insert toolbar displays in menu form—you use a drop-down menu to switch between the eight different iterations of the toolbar (**Figure 9a**).

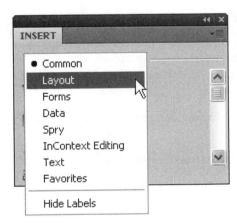

Figure 9a Choosing from the set of Insert toolbar display options.

To view all Insert toolbar tabs at once, dock the Insert toolbar to the top of the Document window (if it is not already there), and choose Show as Tabs from the Insert pop-up menu in the Insert toolbar. In Tab view,

An Alternative: Use the Insert Menu

The Insert menu on the main Dreamweaver CS4 menu bar provides an alternative to using the Insert toolbar. The Insert toolbar allows you to insert frequently used (and even some rarely used) elements like images or tables by clicking icons. The Insert menu provides access to essentially the same set of options but in a menu format. Which is better? It's a matter of preference.

Because the Insert menu accesses a wide range of often-used features in Dreamweaver, a quick survey of that menu will be useful. Many of the features in the Insert menu are, as noted, replicated in other forms (like the Insert toolbar). But some are not. Frequently used (or frequently looked for) features like inserting links, email links, and special characters (like the copyright symbol) are easily accessible from the Insert menu but hard to find elsewhere.

you can easily switch between the eight different toolbars by clicking a tab (**Figure 9b**).

Figure 9b The Insert toolbar displayed as tabs.

While a full survey of the options in the Insert toolbar would amount to a documentation of most of the features available in Dreamweaver, I'll point you to some of the easy-to-access features:

- **Common:** Used to define links, email links, page links (anchors), tables, and media.

- **Layout:** Used to create the three main modes for page design in Dreamweaver—tables, div tags, and layers.

- **Forms:** Used to define input forms, form fields, and form-handling buttons.

- **Data:** Used to insert live data regions in Web sites linked to server-based databases.

- **Spry:** Used to place Spry widgets—JavaScript objects (some with CSS formatting attached) that can be inserted into Web pages to provide interactivity or animation.

- **InContext Editing:** Includes features for managing style sheets and template elements.

- **Text:** Used to apply HTML styles to text and insert special characters.

- **Favorites:** A customizable bar; right-click/Ctrl-click adds features.

#**10** Creating a New Page

There are three basic ways to *edit* the content of a Web page in Dreamweaver's Document window: Code view, Split view, or Design view. Even if you never plan to enter a line of code, it is helpful to understand how these three views work and how to take advantage of them.

Most page designers do most of their work in Design view. Design view allows you to apply page design formatting and add content to your page in an environment that looks like a word processor. As you enter text, embed images, or apply formatting—using graphical design tools—Dreamweaver generates the necessary code (**Figure 10a**).

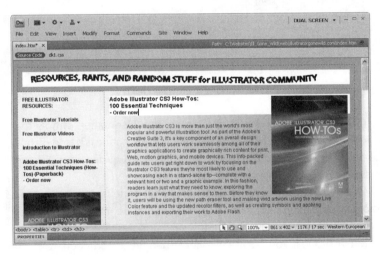

Figure 10a Working in Design view.

The easiest way to see how this works is in Split view. Use the View menu to toggle between turning Split Vertically on or off (to split the Document window horizontally). In Split view, one section of the screen displays generated code, and the other part of the screen displays the graphical design interface (**Figure 10b**).

Create a Site Before Creating a Document

If you are starting a new Web site from scratch, you should define your site before saving Web pages. See Chapter 1, "Creating a Web Site," for information on how to define a local Web site and connect it to a remote site.

Design View vs. Live View

Design view does not provide an interactive preview of your Web page. You can't easily click on and test a link or watch a video. For that, use Live view (see #19, "Testing Pages in Live View").

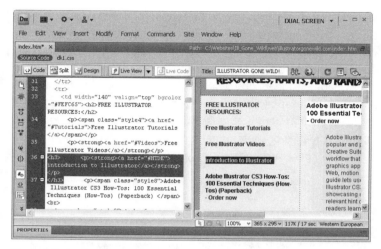

Figure 10b Working in Split view with Split Vertically enabled.

In Design view, Dreamweaver displays a representation of how that code will be interpreted in a browser. This approximation is based on how the Safari browser displays pages, but different browsers and different versions of browsers display code differently.

When you enter code into Code view, that code is translated into a graphical display in Design view. If you enter code into the Code view of the Document window, the Design view updates when you switch to Design view. Or, if you are in Split view, changes to code update in the Design window when you click in the window.

You can create a new Web page in Dreamweaver from either the Files panel or the Document window. Creating a new file in the Files panel simply generates an HTML page, whereas creating a new page in the Document window allows you to define the file type and automatically opens the file in the Document window for editing. To create a new file from the Files panel, go to the Files panel menu and choose File > New File.

Files created from the Files panel menu are named untitled.html (or untitled2.html and so on). You can rename the file in the Files panel by choosing File > Rename from the Files panel menu or by selecting the file in the Files panel and pressing the F2 function key.

Most often, you'll create new files from the Document window. From the Dreamweaver application menu, choose File > New. The New Document dialog opens.

From the far-left column in the New Document dialog, choose Blank Page. From the Page Type list, choose HTML. In the Layout column, select <none>. In the DocType (Document Type; DTD) field, choose the default document type, XHTML 1.0 Transitional. Then click Create to generate a new Web page (**Figure 10c**).

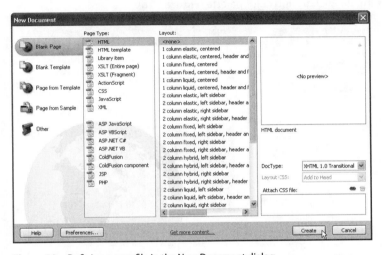

Figure 10c Defining a new file in the New Document dialog.

#11 Defining Page Properties

The Page Properties dialog is a convenient place to define default page font and font size, a default text color, a background color (or image), margins (left, right, top, and bottom), and link display.

To access the Page Properties dialog for an open Web page, choose Modify > Page Properties. The dialog opens with the Appearance (CSS) category selected. Choose a default page font from the Page font pop-up menu. Choose a default text size from the Size pop-up menu. Choose a default text color from the Text color palette and a page background color from the Background color palette (**Figure 11a**).

CSS vs. HTML for Page Properties

The Page Properties dialog has both an Appearance (CSS) category and an Appearance (HTML) category. Using CSS—style sheets—to define page properties is a more powerful and effective technique. CSS provides more formatting options and is more easily adapted to different display environments including mobile devices and display for vision-impaired persons.

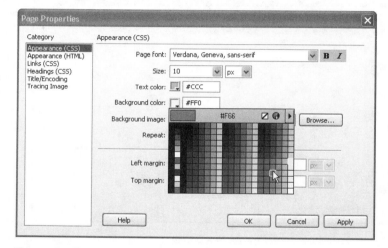

Figure 11a Choosing a page background color.

If you want to use a background image, click the Browse button next to the Background image box to navigate to and select a background image. To tile the background image, choose Repeat from the Repeat pop-up menu. To have your image *not* repeat, choose No-Repeat. To tile the background image vertically only, choose Repeat-Y, and to tile the image horizontally only, choose Repeat-X (**Figure 11b**).

Different browsers handle page margins differently, but if you want to be sure no margins display around your page, enter 0 (zero) in the Left margin, Right margin, Top margin, and Bottom margin boxes in the Appearance (CSS) category in the Page Properties dialog (**Figure 11c**).

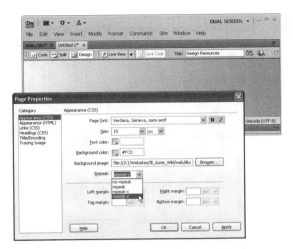

Figure 11b Tiling a page background image vertically.

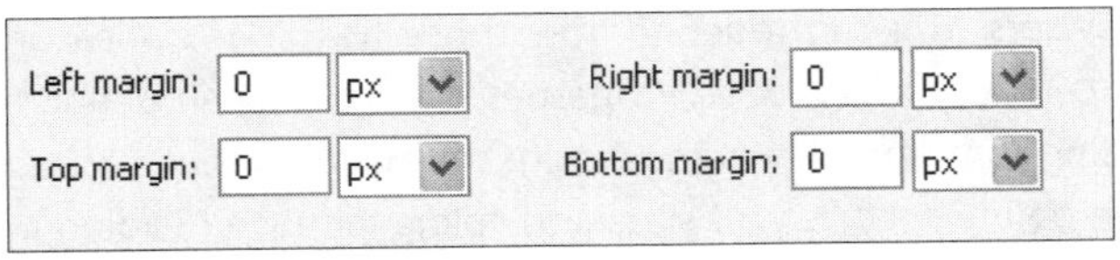

| Left margin: | 0 | px | | Right margin: | 0 | px | |
| Top margin: | 0 | px | | Bottom margin: | 0 | px | |

Figure 11c Defining no margins for a Web page.

By default, unfollowed links display as underlined blue, followed links as underlined purple, and active (open) links as underlined red. You can change the settings for your page using the options in the Links category in the Page Properties dialog. And, you can define a special rollover state that displays when a visitor moves his or her mouse cursor over a link.

To define link appearance, click the Links category in the Page Properties dialog. Generally, it is not a good idea to change the Link font or size, since it is distracting to have text change font or size when displaying as a link. Choose link colors for all four link states using the palettes.

To change the underline style for your links, choose one of the four options from the Underline style pop-up menu (**Figure 11d**).

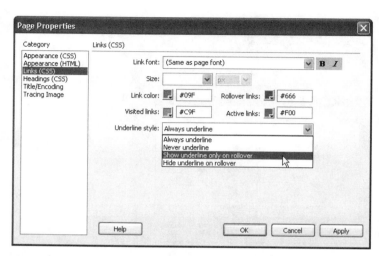

Figure 11d Choosing to underline links in a rollover state only.

There are six standard HTML Heading tags that are universally interpreted by browsers. You can redefine how those headings appear in the Headings category in the Page Properties dialog. You can define a different heading font (for all headings) from the Heading font pop-up menu. You can define specific font sizes and colors for each heading in the individual boxes next to each heading (**Figure 11e**).

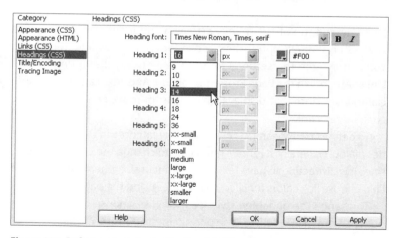

Figure 11e Defining a font size for Heading 1 HTML tags on a page.

After you have defined page properties, click Apply to see how they look on your open page. Click OK to save the page property definitions.

#12 Defining Links

Links are one of the most basic and dynamic elements of a Web page. In fact, hypertext, the H in HTML, refers to text that could have link properties (at least at the time the name was coined). Links can be associated with text or images.

Generally speaking, link targets can be one of two types: relative (internal to your site) or absolute (outside your site). Both are defined in the Property inspector for selected text (or a selected image).

To define an absolute link, start by selecting the text you want to link from. In the Property inspector, click the HTML button if that is not selected (deselect the CSS button). With the text selected, you can type an absolute link in the Link box in the Property inspector (**Figure 12a**).

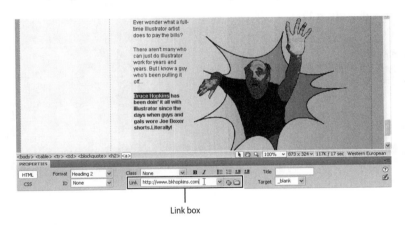

Link box

Figure 12a Entering an absolute-link target for selected text.

With relative links, you don't define where the link is found on the Internet; you define where the link is located relative to the current page—and at your Web site.

To define a relative link, with the link text selected, click the blue Browse for File icon next to the Link box in the Property inspector. The Select File dialog opens. Navigate to the linked file, and click Choose to generate a link to that file. The relative link appears in the Link box in the Property inspector (**Figure 12b**).

Browse for File

Figure 12b Defining a relative link.

The other attribute that is important to define for a link is the Target window. By default, links open in the *same* browser window as the linking page, causing the linking page to disappear. A visitor can click the Back button on his or her browser to return to the original, linking page.

If you want a page to open in a *new* browser window, go to the Property inspector and choose the _blank attribute in the Target pop-up menu (**Figure 12c**).

Figure 12c Defining the _blank link target that will open the link in a new browser window.

#13 Defining Email Links

To convert text with an email address into an email link, simply select the text and choose Insert > Email Link. The Email Link dialog appears, and the text you selected is automatically identified as the email link (**Figure 13a**).

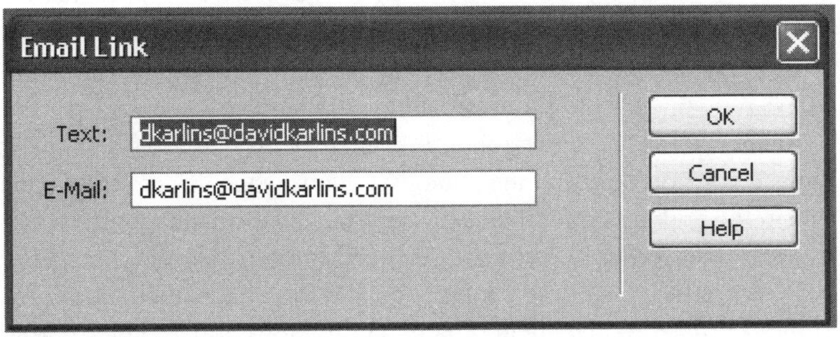

Figure 13a Defining an email link from selected text.

Or, you can select any text (or image) and define that as an email link. To do so, first select the text or image that will serve as the email link. Then choose Insert > Email Link. The Email Link dialog appears.

If you selected text as an email link, that text appears in the Text box in the Email Link dialog. Type the email address for the link into the E-Mail box (**Figure 13b**).

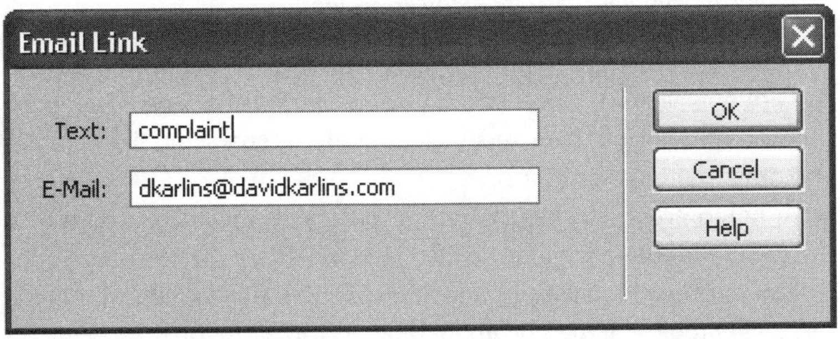

Figure 13b Creating an email link.

#14 Saving Files

Page Filename and Page Title

Every Web page has both a filename and a page title. The *filename* is the way the file is identified and located within a Web site.

Page *titles* describe the page content for visitors. They *can* contain special characters, including punctuation and spaces.

After you create a new page, you need to *save* it with a *filename,* and you need to assign a page *title* to that page. Every Web page needs a filename and a title. The filename is mainly an internal element. It is used to locate the file in a Web site and to link the file to other files. As such, filenames don't have to be very creative, but they should avoid special characters like commas, ampersands (&), percent signs (%), spaces, and so on. You'll be safe if you stick to lowercase alphanumeric characters, plus the helpful dash (-) and underscore (_) characters.

There is a special requirement for filenames assigned to a site home page. A site home page is the page that opens when visitors enter your URL in the address bar of their browser. This URL does not specify a file, only a server location. Once the server location is open in a browser, browsers detect the home page by looking for a file named index.htm or index.html. *Never* create files named both index.htm and index.html; this will confuse your server, the browsers, and you. Instead, choose one or the other, and create a file called index.html (or index.htm). This will be your home page.

Note
You can create files with the same name but with different filename extensions (like index.htm and index.html, for example). But don't! Web browsers will recognize either .htm or .html as a Web page filename extension, but they will get confused if you have Web pages with the same name and different versions of the extension.

Pages titles are different from page filenames. Titles have nothing to do with how files are saved, linked to, or managed at a server. Therefore, they can contain any characters, including special characters like commas and other punctuation marks.

As noted, *every* page has a page title, but unless you assign a page title, the default "Untitled Page" page title appears in browser title bars.

You can enter (or change) page title information in the Title field in the Document toolbar. If the Document toolbar is not visible in the Document window, choose View > Toolbars > Document (**Figure 14a**).

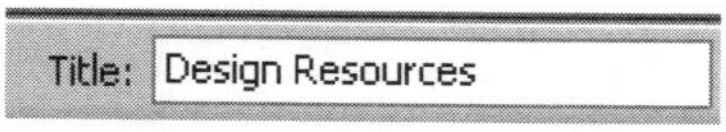

Title: Design Resources

Figure 14a Entering a page title.

Page titles display in a browser title bar. Therefore, you should make them helpful and descriptive. When you save a page for the first time, you name the page by entering a filename. With a file open in the Save As dialog in the Document window, choose File > Save and enter a filename in the File Name field (**Figure 14b**).

Figure 14b Saving and naming a Web page.

#15 Using Blank Page Layouts

Dreamweaver CS4 provides a number of predesigned page layouts that you can customize with your own content. They use CSS (style sheet) coding to define boxes on the pages.

Blank templates do not provide content. They just provide page designs, and you supply all the content.

To select one of the blank templates, choose File > New, and then choose Blank Page from the list of categories on the left side of the New Document dialog. In the Page Type column, choose HTML.

You preview each of the page designs by choosing one in the Layout column of the New Document dialog and inspecting the layout in the preview area in the upper-right corner of the dialog (**Figure 15a**).

Can You Edit Blank Page Layouts?

You can easily edit the *content* of blank page layouts. However, these layouts are really best if used as is without adjusting the actual layout.

You can edit the CSS-defined page objects, but doing that requires some facility with using CSS layout div tags, which are discussed in #33, "Editing Layout Div Tags in the CSS Styles Panel." That said, if you're comfortable enough editing CSS div tags, you can just as easily create your own CSS designed pages, and you won't need the blank page layouts supplied by Dreamweaver CS4. There are enough blank page layouts available to satisfy most design needs, so you'll likely find a layout close to what you need without any tweaking.

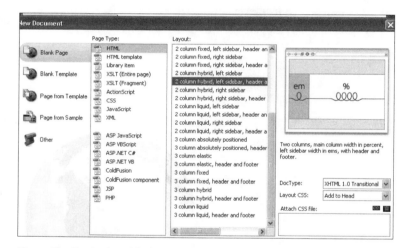

Figure 15a Previewing a blank page layout.

Once you select a blank template to use as a framework for your page design, you can accept the rest of the default settings in the New Document dialog, and then click Create to generate a new page. That page still needs to be saved with a filename after you add your own content to it (**Figure 15b**).

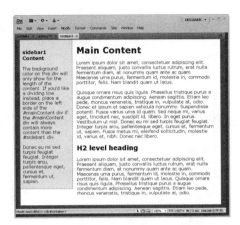

Figure 15b A page generated from the "2 column elastic, left sidebar" blank page layout.

Elastic, Liquid, and Fixed

Blank page layouts have columns divided using elastic, liquid, or fixed dividers. Fixed column widths are a set number of pixels. They do not resize. Elastic column width is set in ems and changes relative to the size of the text. Liquid column width is a percentage of the visitor's browser window. Hybrid columns are open or another mix of elastic, liquid, and fixed column widths.

When you generate a new page from a blank layout, the default document type setting is XHTML 1.0 Transitional. This is a highly flexible, supported page format and generally you will not want to change this setting unless your Web administrator has mandated a different document type standard.

You also have options for how to handle the Layout CSS used to define your page layout. The CSS code for generated pages from blank layouts is, by default, added to the top of the Web page. Of course, this code is not visible in browsers, but it defines the page layout. You can, alternatively, elect to generate a *new* CSS page with the layout coding that is linked to your generated HTML page. This is more complex but allows the CSS content to be attached to multiple pages. For a full discussion of embedding CSS in pages or linking it via an external style sheet file, see Chapter 5, "Designing Pages with Absolute Placement Objects."

You can choose the default option of adding CSS to the HTML page by choosing Add to Head from the Layout CSS pop-up menu in the New Document dialog. Or, you can generate a separate, linked CSS page by choosing Create New File from the Layout CSS pop-up menu. (**Figure 15c**).

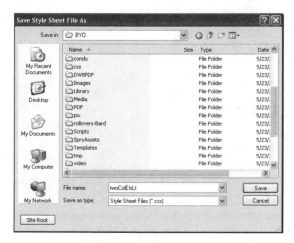

Figure 15c Saving blank page CSS as a separate, linked CSS file.

#16 Creating Blank Templates

Dreamweaver templates are special pages that are used only to generate other pages. They contain both editable and noneditable regions. The editable parts of the template are customized for individual pages, whereas the noneditable parts remain the same on every page associated with the templates. Using templates to manage large Web sites is a powerful technique for ensuring uniformity in style and for facilitating global updating. Managing Web sites using templates is explored in #48, "Creating Template Pages."

Here, you will briefly look at how Dreamweaver's New Document window allows you to generate new page templates.

To create a new template, choose File > New and choose Blank Template from the list of categories on the left side of the New Document dialog. In the Template Type column, choose ASP JavaScript template. The ASP and JavaScript templates are the most widely compatible with different hosting and browsing environments.

The process of creating a new blank template is very similar to creating a blank page from a layout. Choose File > New, and then select Blank Template from the category column on the left. You can preview each of the page design ("blank") templates by choosing one in the Layout column in the New Document dialog and inspecting the layout in the preview area in the upper-right corner of the dialog (**Figure 16a**).

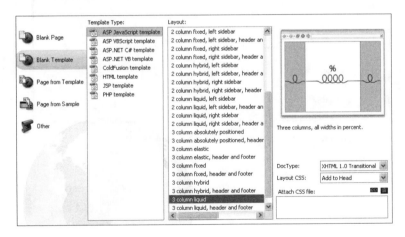

Figure 16a Previewing a blank template.

Once you select a blank template layout, you can accept the rest of the default settings in the New Document dialog and click Create to generate a new page.

That page will then be saved not as a regular Web page but as a template. With the new template page open, choose File > Save. Since you have not at this point defined editable regions, a dialog will alert you that there are no editable regions. Click OK and the Save As Template dialog opens. In the Save As Template dialog, select a site from the Site pop-up menu to define which of your Dreamweaver sites will access this template. You can also enter a description for the template in the Description box. Enter a name for the template in the Save as box. When the file is saved, a .dwt filename extension will be added to the filename, and the file will be saved in the Templates folder of your site. This folder is automatically generated by Dreamweaver (**Figure 16b**).

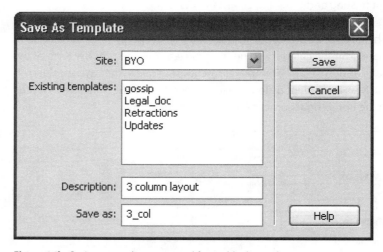

Figure 16b Saving a template generated from a blank template.

#17 Creating Pages from Other Sources

A number of online sources are available for predesigned page layouts. TemplateMonster.com, for example, provides many useful ready-to-download pages. These pages download as a single archived file, which you then extract into a folder on your computer.

To edit a page from a source like TemplateMonster.com, choose File > Open and navigate to the folder in which you saved the downloaded page or pages (**Figure 17**).

Figure 17 Opening a downloaded sample page.

After you open the page in the Document window, you can edit and save it. Save the page by choosing File > Save As, and then save the page in the folder that contains your site content. When you save the page, you will likely be prompted to update links in the page because you are moving it to a new folder. You may also be prompted to save associated files, including images and associated CSS (formatting) files, into the folder on your computer for your Web site.

#18 Creating Pages from Sample Style Sheets

Pages from Samples Are CSS Files

To be clear, pages from samples are *not* generated HTML pages—they are predesigned *style sheets*. The files that are generated from these sample style sheets must be attached— either by linking or by importing—to an HTML page.

Dreamweaver CS4 provides a set of sample style sheets that define elements like text font, text color, link attributes, and heading styles.

When you create a file from the Page from Samples category, you are *not* creating a Web page or a starter Web page of any kind. You are simply saving a CSS styles file that can be applied to pages.

To generate a CSS file from a sample CSS style, follow these steps:

1. Choose File > New, and then choose Page from Sample from the category list on the left side of the New Document dialog.

2. In the Sample Folder column, choose CSS Style Sheet.

3. Explore the available style sheets in the Sample Page column. Note that what you see in the preview area in the upper right of the New Document dialog is *only the formatting* that will be applied. The content in these previews will not be generated as part of the CSS file (**Figure 18a**).

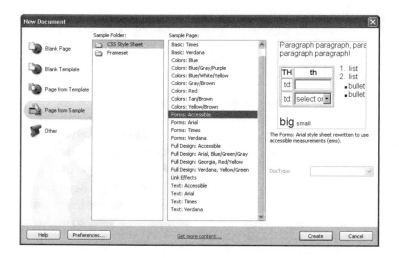

Figure 18a Previewing a style sheet.

4. When you find a style you want to save as a CSS page, click Create. A CSS file will open in the document window. This file is not "previewable" because it only includes formatting code, not page content (**Figure 18b**).

```
body {
    background-color: #FFFFFF;
    font-family: Arial, Helvetica, sans-serif;
    font-size: 1em;
    margin-top: 0.1em;
    margin-right: 0.1em;
    margin-bottom: 0.1em;
    margin-left: 0.1em;
    }
form {
    font-family: Arial, Helvetica, sans-serif;
    font-size: 1em
    }
h2 {
    color: #CCCCCC
    }
h3 {
    color: #CCCCCC
    }
h4 {
    color: #000000
    }
input {
    font-family: Arial, Helvetica, sans-serif;
    font-size: 1em
    }
li {
    font-family: Arial, Helvetica, sans-serif;
    font-size: 1em
```

Figure 18b A generated CSS page in the Document window.

5. Save the CSS file by choosing File > Save. By default, the file will have a .css (not .htm or .html) filename extension.

6. After you have saved the sample CSS page, you can import that formatting into any open HTML page. Create or open an existing HTML page and view the CSS panel. Click the Attach Style Sheet icon at the bottom of the CSS Styles panel (it looks like a link icon) (**Figure 18c**).

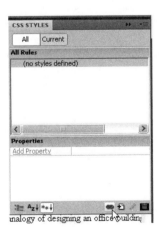

Figure 18c Using the Attach Style Sheet icon to attach a sample style sheet.

(continued on next page)

#18: Creating Pages from Sample Style Sheets

7. The Attach External Style Sheet dialog opens. Click the Browse button to locate the CSS file you saved in step 5, and then click Choose in the Select Style Sheet File dialog. The CSS file is now listed in the File/URL box in the Attach External Style Sheet dialog (**Figure 18d**).

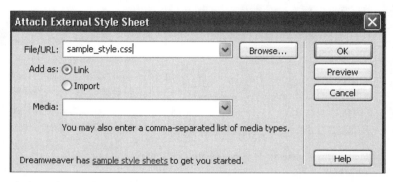

Figure 18d Attaching an external style sheet.

8. In the Attach External Style Sheet dialog, choose Import in the Add as options area, and then click OK. The styles will be applied to your open page.

#**19** Testing Pages in Live View

When you work in Design view, you can edit page content, but you cannot test links. And, generally speaking, you do not really see pages as they will appear in a browser.

Live view allows you to see your page as it *will* appear in a browser. However, for that very reason, you cannot edit page content in Live view. For example, if you click on a link in Design view, you can edit that link but not follow it. If you click on a link in Live view, you can follow the link but not edit it.

To view a page in Live view, choose View > Live View (**Figure 19a**).

Figure 19a Toggling from Design view to Live view.

In Live view, you can test links, enter data into forms, and generally interact with your Web page just as you would in a browser (**Figure 19b**).

For hand coders, Live view offers the option of being able to split your screen, enter and edit HTML and other code in Code view, and then in another split screen, examine and test the results in a browser-like environment. To set that up, click the Split icon in the Document toolbar, and then

Testing Forms in Live View

As with links, you cannot test a form in Design view. However, in Live view, you can enter data in a form and test the form.

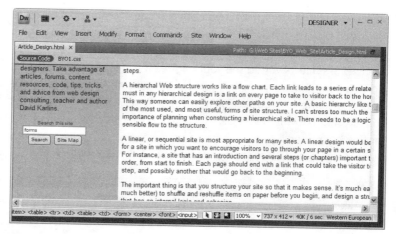

Figure 19b Testing a form in Live view.

click the Live view icon. The Live Code icon in the Document toolbar must be deselected in order to edit code. With Code view in one window and Live view in another, you can edit code. You can then click the Refresh Design View icon in the Document toolbar to see your edited code reflected in Live view, where you can test it in a browser (**Figure 19c**).

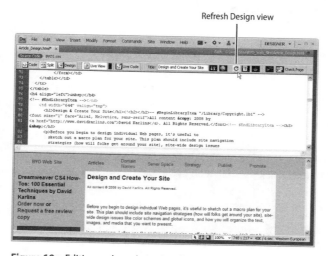

Refresh Design view

Figure 19c Editing code and viewing the result in Live view.

CHAPTER THREE

Creating and Formatting Tables

The use of tables as a design tool has been partly supplanted by the evolving ability to design more complex, flexible, and in some ways accessible Web pages using CSS (page design with CSS in Dreamweaver CS4 is explored in Chapter 5, "Designing Pages with Absolute Placement Objects). Still, tables remain a stable, reliable, and universally supported technique for page design, and are even used in combination with CSS in page design.

Also, with the addition of Spry Data Sets to Dreamweaver CS4, tables take on new importance in Dreamweaver as a form of organizing data. Table data can now be updated in a table and displayed live in other Dreamweaver Web pages. For a full exploration of how to use tables to manage live data in Dreamweaver—including a model for designing a table used as a database—see Chapter 14, "Using Spry Data Sets."

#20 Creating a Table

A basic, useful, and safe way to design a Web page is to first define a single-cell table, and then place page content inside that cell. Constraining page content in a rectangular table—especially constraining page *width* using a table—allows you to control the width at which your page displays in a browser. Creating a one-cell table is also a useful way of familiarizing yourself with the basic concepts involved in Web page design with tables.

To create a one-cell table for page content, follow these steps:

1. Open a new page. Choose File > New and select the Blank Page category and HTML in the New Document dialog; then click Create.

   With the new page open, your cursor is in the upper-left corner of the page by default. Insert a new table at the cursor using the following steps.

2. Choose Insert > Table from the Document window menu. The Table dialog appears.

   Tip
   Alternatively, you can click the Table button in the Layout panel of the Insert toolbar. See Chapter 2, "Creating Web Pages," #9, "Using the Insert Toolbar," for an explanation of how to use the different tabs in the Insert toolbar. The Table button is also in the Common panel of the Insert toolbar.

3. In the Rows and Columns boxes, define the number of rows and columns in your table. It's easy to add rows and columns later, so when in doubt, simply generate a one-row, one-column table by entering 1 in both the Rows and Columns boxes.

4. In the Table width box, enter a value representing either a number of pixels or a percentage of page width. Then choose either pixels or percent from the Table width pop-up menu (**Figure 20**). For more on this, see #22, "Creating Fixed and Flexible Columns."

5. The Border thickness box defines the width of the displayed border. Normally, tables used for page layout are defined with no border displayed. To display no border around a table, enter 0 (zero) in the Border thickness box. Or, to display a border, enter a value such as 1 (for 1 pixel).

Layout Mode Is Gone—Expanded Tables Mode Remains

With Dreamweaver CS4, Layout mode has been removed as an option for designing pages with tables, and instead, all tables are created in what was formally called standard mode.

You can choose Expanded Tables Mode in Dreamweaver CS4. Expanded Tables view makes it easier to select a table or a cell by displaying exaggerated borders around cells and the table for easier clicking. Choose View > Table Mode > Expanded Tables Mode to display this view.

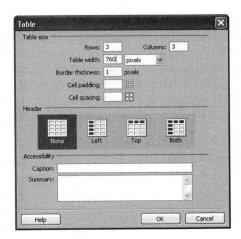

Figure 20 Defining table width in pixels.

Tip

Table border color is defined in the Property inspector—see #23, "Defining Table Properties."

6. The Cell padding and Cell spacing boxes define the distance between cells and the padding inside a cell. Cell padding defines the buffer between cell content (like text or images) and the cell border. Cell spacing defines the spacing between cells. To define padding, enter a value (the unit of measurement is pixels) in the Cell padding box. To define spacing (around the outside of the single-cell table), enter a value in the Cell spacing box.

Tip

A useful and often-used setting is to define 6 pixels of cell padding and 0 pixels of cell spacing. This prevents cell content from bumping into content in the adjoining cell, but at the same time eliminates the table "showing through" between cells, which is the point of defining cell spacing.

7. The Header and Accessibility areas in the Table dialog define features that are used by screen readers—software programs that read Web pages out loud to people who cannot read screen content. These tools are not particularly important or useful if you are using your table as a display tool. So, when defining a single-cell table for page layout, leave these areas blank.

Displaying Table Borders

Normally, tables used for design purposes are created with no border width. To ensure that browsers understand that you do not want to display borders, enter a 0 in the Border thickness box in the Table dialog: Don't rely on leaving the box blank.

Even though table borders are often defined to not display in a browser, you normally *do* want to see them in the Dreamweaver Document window. Otherwise, it's difficult to know where the table is and where to enter content into the table.

By default, Dreamweaver displays table borders—even those with no width—in the Document window. To change the setting or to toggle back to display table borders if this feature is disabled, choose View > Visual Aids > Table Borders.

Note

The Header and Accessibility areas are useful if you are presenting large amounts of table data. In that case, left and/or top headers "announce" the nature of the content in the associated row (in the case of left headers) or column (in the case of top headers). Similarly, table captions and summaries are not necessary or helpful if you are using a table for page layout, but they can be helpful if you are presenting data that will be read out loud by reader software.

After you define a table in the Table dialog, click OK to generate the table. You will see the table displayed in the Document window even if you defined it with no border.

Even if your Web page doesn't require intricate design, you can constrain the display width of your Web page in a table. Placing content in a table enables you to define the width of your page in a browser. Without a table to constrain width (either to a fixed number of pixels or to a percentage of the browser window width), the page content will expand horizontally to fill the browser window. In many cases, that will make the text lines too long to be readable.

Experts differ over optimum page width, but the consensus is that a 760-pixel-wide table provides a convenient, accessible, and attractive framework for presenting text and images in a browser window.

Page *height* is normally not defined in a table, because if table width is fixed, the content must have a direction in which it can expand if a viewer's browsing environment enlarges the content. This happens when a visitor's screen displays a lower resolution (causing images to expand on the screen), when type font size is increased, or for other reasons.

There are two basic approaches to using a table to constrain page width—percent and pixels. Choosing a percent produces a table that is a set proportion of a browser window width. A setting of 75%, for example, will fill three quarters of a viewer's browser window with your Web page.

Defining table width in pixels allows you more control over how a page displays. Choosing a 760-pixel-wide table, for example, produces a Web page that is about 8 inches wide in typical computer monitor resolutions.

Combining fixed-width columns with a flexible-width column in some ways is the best of both worlds. Some content (like navigation bars) can be constrained to fixed widths, whereas other content (like large blocks of text) can stretch horizontally so that the page fills all or most of the browser window.

#21 Importing Data as Tables

Dreamweaver CS4 makes it easy to create a Web page table from either an Excel spreadsheet (this feature is available in the Windows version only) or delimited text. A delimited text file is a text file (in a program like Microsoft Word or any text editor) in which columns of data are separated by tabs, commas, colons, semicolons, or other characters.

To import an Excel document into an open Web page as a table, choose File > Import > Excel Document. The Insert Excel Document dialog opens. Navigate to and select an Excel file, and then click Open to insert the Excel worksheet into your Web page as an HTML table (**Figure 21a**).

Figure 21a Selecting an Excel table to embed in a Web page.

Once imported into a Web page, the Excel spreadsheet is a regular HTML table, and you can use all the formatting techniques discussed in this chapter to adjust page widths, resize the table, format background colors, and so on (**Figure 21b**).

TITLE	PRICE	URL
Adobe Illustrator CS3 How-Tos: 100 Essential Techniques	$19.79	http://www.amazon.com/Adobe-Illustrator-CS3-How-Tos-Techniques/dp/0321508947/ref=sr_1_1?ie=UTF8&s=books&qid=1215459478&sr=1-1
Adobe Dreamweaver CS3 How-Tos: 100 Essential Techniques	$19.79	http://www.amazon.com/Adobe-Dreamweaver-CS3-How-Tos-Techniques/dp/0321508939/ref=sr_1_2?ie=UTF8&s=books&qid=1215459478&sr=1-2
Digital Sports Photography : Take Winning Shots Every Time	$19.79	http://www.amazon.com/Digital-Sports-Photography-Winning-Shots/dp/0764596607/ref=sr_1_3?ie=UTF8&s=books&qid=1215459478&sr=1-3
Enhancing a Dreamweaver CS3 Web Site with Flash Video: Visual QuickProject Guide	$14.98	http://www.amazon.com/Enhancing-Dreamweaver-Site-Flash-Video/dp/0321535235/ref=sr_1_5?ie=UTF8&s=books&qid=1215459478&sr=1-5

Figure 21b An imported Excel worksheet embedded as a table in a Web page (this feature is available for Windows only).

To import a delimited text file as a table, choose Insert > Table Objects > Import Tabular Data. The Import Tabular dialog opens. Use the Browse button next to the Data File box to navigate to and select a text file. Use the Delimiter pop-up menu to choose the character used to separate fields (columns) in your data file. In the Table Width area in the Import Tabular Data dialog, you can choose Fit to Data, or you can choose the Set To option to define a width for the generated table, either in percent or pixels.

Use the Cell Padding box to define spacing within each cell between the content and the outside of the cell. Use the Cell Spacing box to define spacing between cells. Use the Border box to define the thickness of cell borders (choose 0 for no visible border). If the top row of the imported data has column headings, you can choose separate formatting (like Bold) for that top row (**Figure 21c**).

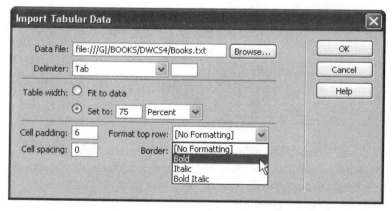

Figure 21c Importing tabular data.

#22 Creating Fixed and Flexible Columns

A widely used and very functional technique for page design involves creating tables that combine fixed columns with a flexible column. Very frequently, Web pages are built around tables that have locked (fixed-width) left and right columns and a center column that expands to fill a specified percent of a browser window.

For example, a table might provide a 100-pixel-wide column on the left side of the page for navigation, a 100-pixel-wide column on the right, and a flexible column that fills all the remaining available space in a browser window (**Figure 22a**).

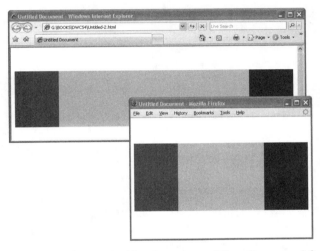

Figure 22a Fixed and flexible columns in two different browsers—left and right column widths are fixed, but the center column is flexible in width.

Use the steps that follow to create a Web page with two fixed-width columns and one flexible-width column.

1. Create a new three-column table by choosing Insert > Table. In the Table dialog, enter 3 in the Columns box and enter 1 in the Rows box.

2. Set Table width to 100%.

(continued on next page)

3. Set Border thickness to 0, Cell padding to 6, and Cell spacing to 0. Click OK to generate a three-column table that will fill 100% of a browser window (**Figure 22b**). Click OK to generate the table.

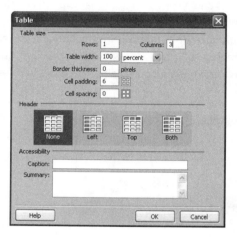

Figure 22b Defining a three-column table that fills 100% of a browser window.

4. Select the left column in the table by clicking in it or on top of it (**Figure 22c**).

Tip

Column width is explained in more detail in #23, "Defining Table Properties." As explained there, height and width are usually defined in pixels, which is the default setting in the Property inspector.

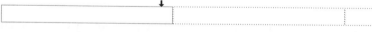

Figure 22c Selecting the left column.

Tip

If the Property inspector is not visible, press Ctrl/Command+F3.

5. Enter 100 in the W (Width) box in the Property inspector (**Figure 22d**).

Figure 22d Assigning a 100-pixel width to a selected table column.

6. Repeat steps 4 and 5, but select the right column and set the width to 100 pixels.

Tip

Locking column widths only ensures that the width of the column does not get smaller than the set amount of pixels. If you place a large image in a column, the column will expand to accommodate the width of that image.

You can now add content to the columns you defined. When the page is viewed in a browser, the middle column will expand or contract horizontally when the width of the browser window is changed.

#23 Defining Table Properties

Table properties include elements like height, width, cell spacing, cell padding, border width and color, and background color or image. All these features can be defined in the Property inspector.

The trick is to select a *table,* not a cell. With the table selected, the Property inspector allows you to define table properties, and with a cell selected you can define cell properties (see #24, "Formatting Cells," for details) (**Figure 23**).

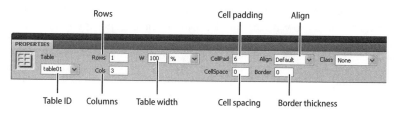

Figure 23 The Property inspector with a table selected.

Table ID is used when the table is controlled by scripts (like a JavaScript animation) and to apply style properties using CSS style sheets. The Class pop-up menu is used to apply CSS styles to the table.

These are the critical options in the Property inspector:

- The Rows and Cols boxes define (or change) how many rows or columns are in a table. Adding to the existing number adds a row below the bottom row or a column to the right of the last existing column. Decreasing the value deletes rows or columns starting from the right or bottom of the table.

- Table width (W) and height (H) can be defined in pixels or percent. Normally, table height is not defined, because it will vary depending on the amount of content in the table.

- CellPad defines space (in pixels) between the border of a cell and cell content. CellSpace defines space (in pixels) between cells.

- The Align options pop-up menu places the table on the left (default), right, or center of the page.

#24 Formatting Cells

When you click inside a table cell, the bottom half of the Property inspector displays properties for the selected cell. This works the same whether the CSS or the HTML button is selected in the Property inspector (features for formatting the *content* of a cell are different in HTML and CSS, and those different features display in the top half of the Property inspector). With a cell selected, you can format that cell. The Property inspector also allows you to merge selected cells or split a cell.

The Property inspector that appears for a selected cell displays formatting options for type (or other selected objects, like an image) in the top section. In the bottom section, you define cell properties (**Figure 24a**).

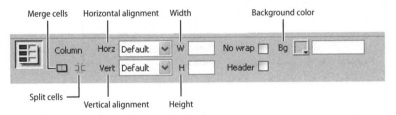

Figure 24a The Property inspector for a selected cell or cells.

To set a cell width, enter a value in the Width box. To set cell height, enter a value in the Height box. You can also adjust cell height and width by simply clicking and dragging the divider between cell rows or columns (**Figure 24b**).

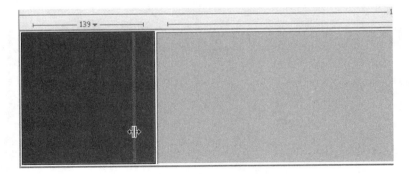

Figure 24b Change column width by dragging the divider between columns.

Select a Cell Easily

You might find it easier to select a cell with Expanded Tables Mode on (Choose View > Table Mode > Expanded Tables Mode).

Expanding the Property Inspector

If you can't see the bottom section of the Property inspector, click the Expand (down-pointing) triangle in the lower-right corner of the Property inspector.

To combine cells, click and drag to select contiguous (touching) cells, and click the Merge cells button in the Property inspector. To split a cell, select the cell, and click the Split cell button in the Property inspector. The Split Cell dialog appears, allowing you to define how cells are split (**Figure 24c**).

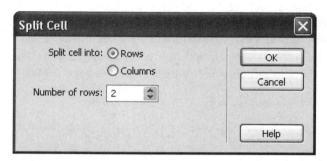

Figure 24c Splitting cells.

The No Wrap check box in the Property inspector for a selected cell (or cells) prevents text in a cell from wrapping (forcing line breaks) at the border of the cell. The Header check box defines a cell as a header—an attribute that when applied to the top row in a table can contribute to accessibility in some browsing environments.

#25 Embedding Tables Within Tables

Many page designs can be created by dividing a table into rows and columns. More complex page layouts might require embedding tables inside other tables. One reason for this is that there are properties of a table that apply to *all* cells in a table—specifically, cell spacing and padding. That means that every cell within that table will inherit the spacing and padding properties of the *table*. If you want to create cells within a table that do *not* inherit the properties of the table, you can do this by embedding a new table with different table properties. For example, there may be times when you need to combine page elements enclosed in a table with no buffer (a banner on the top of a page for instance) with page elements that are in columns buffered with spacing between cells (**Figure 25a**).

Figure 25a A page design with a table embedded within a master table.

There are a couple of tricks involved in embedding a table within a table. The following steps will walk you through the process safe and sound:

1. Create the first table with one column, one row, no border, no cell spacing, and no cell padding. See #20, "Creating a Table," for details. Set the width of the table with a value in pixels or percent. This value will set the outside limits of the page width, and all tables you embed within your table will be no wider than the width you define here. Click OK to generate the table.

2. To see the table and table elements clearly as you embed tables within it, choose Expanded Tables Mode. Do this by clicking the Expand icon in the Insert toolbar or by choosing View > Table Mode > Expanded Tables Mode. A more easily visible and selectable border appears around the single-cell table.

3. As you insert tables within the table, you are actually inserting them within that table's single *cell*. Vertical alignment in tables is defined by

Embedded Table Scenario

A clean way to design a tables-based Web page would be to create one "master" table with no cell spacing or cell padding. At the top of the table, you could then embed a second table, a one 1-column table with no cell padding or spacing. Under that embedded table, you could embed another table with three columns and content separated by 6 pixels of cell spacing that would serve as placeholders for navigation content (on the left), main page text (in the middle), and additional material (the right column).

cell. Click in the cell and choose Top in the Vert (Vertical) field in the Property inspector (**Figure 25b**).

Tip

Different cells in a table can have different vertical alignments. Oddly enough, the default vertical alignment setting for cells is middle—so content drops to the middle of the cell as you enter it. Here you want the vertical cell alignment set to Top so that content fills columns from the top.

Figure 25b Setting vertical alignment to Top.

4. With your cursor still in the single cell of the table, choose Insert > Table. Now you can define any table properties you desire—choose a number of columns and rows, define borders, and set cell padding or spacing. The only trick is that if you want your embedded table to fill the table in which it is placed, you need to set the width to 100%.

5. Select the embedded table by clicking the embedded table border. Press the right arrow key on your keyboard to place the insertion point just to the right of the embedded table. Choose Insert > Table to place a new table and define table properties. Here, again, you will probably want to set the width of the second embedded table to 100%.

CHAPTER FOUR

Using Framesets

Frames allow you to display more than one Web page in a browser window. You can accomplish this by generating a special kind of Web page that has no content of its own but simply serves as a container to display other Web pages that are embedded in *frames* within that container page. The whole *set* of HTML pages that work together to present more than one page in a browser is referred to as a *frameset*.

There are distinct advantages to designing with frames. Since each frame within a frameset is a separate Web page, visitors can scroll (usually vertically) within one frame while continuing to view content undisturbed in a separate frame.

There are also real disadvantages to designing with frames. One is that search engines do not organize pages by framesets but instead produce page results that direct searchers to a *page,* not a frameset. This means that people will come to pages that were intended to be displayed within a frameset, but those pages will be individual pages.

Another disadvantage to framesets is that they can pose accessibility issues for visitors using screen reader software, usually vision-impaired people who rely on devices other than a mouse to navigate online. A solution to these accessibility issues is to provide a "frameless" alternative to any frameset at your site.

#26 Generating a Frameset

Frames Reduce Download Time

Frames can help reduce download time for Web pages, because page content in one frame does not have to reload when new content is displayed in another frame.

A typical and useful implementation of frames is a two-frame page design in which the left frame serves as a navigation section of the page and the right (and larger) frame displays page content.

One advantage of this setup is that it allows visitors to scroll vertically down a long set of navigation links while much larger content displays in a wider frame on the right side of the page (**Figure 26a**).

Figure 26a Digital designer Bruce K. Hopkins uses a frameset to allow visitors to scroll through thumbnails in one frame and see larger images in another.

One downside to designing with frames is that managing files is at least three times as confusing as working with a normal page. That's in part because each frameset includes at least three HTML pages: one to serve as the overall frameset and at least two framed pages embedded in the frameset. The best way to manage this challenge is to generate framesets from a set of sample pages.

To see the set of sample frames, choose File > New, and then choose Page from Sample in the category list on the left side of the New Document dialog. In the Sample Folder column, choose Frameset. Preview predesigned framesets in the preview area in the upper right of the dialog (**Figure 26b**).

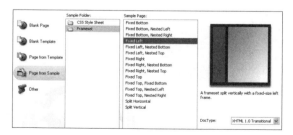

Figure 26b Selecting the Fixed Left sample frameset.

After you generate a frameset from a sample in the New Document window, the Frame Tag Accessibility Attributes dialog appears. Here, you assign names to all the frames in the frameset. Naming frames is *different* than naming the HTML files in a frameset. You'll be prompted to do both, so don't get confused by this. The frame name is useful in defining link targets and other frame attributes, and must be defined separately. Normally, the default frame names in the dialog are fine (these names are not visible in browsers), so go ahead and OK each Frame Tag Accessibility Attribute dialog that appears when you generate a frameset (**Figure 26c**).

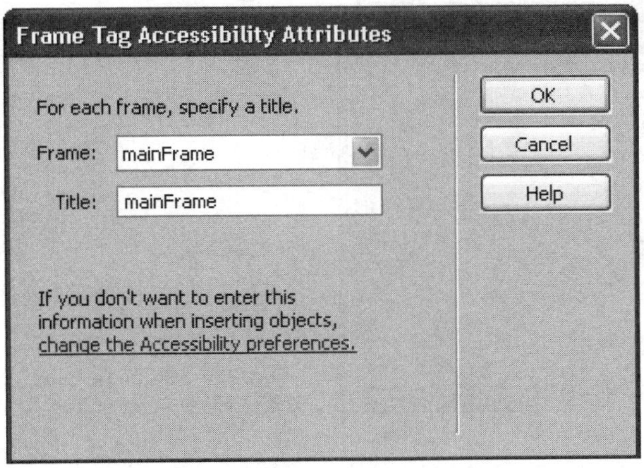

Figure 26c Assigning a frame name to frames.

To save a frameset, choose File > Save All from the main Dreamweaver window. You will be saving at least three files: the frameset file and each embedded page within the frameset.

You can edit the content of that frameset, and you can edit the formatting of the frameset. That process is explained in #27, "Formatting Framesets."

Frames and Search Engines

Another significant disadvantage of designing with frames is that frames tend to confuse search engines, which identify content in HTML pages, not in combined frames. Visitors might end up following a search link to an HTML Web page that is intended to be displayed within a frame, and therefore see only part of the page content. Frames also pose accessibility problems for visitors with handheld browsing devices.

However, because frames open up design possibilities that cannot be easily accomplished with other page design techniques, they remain a viable element of page design.

#27 Formatting Framesets

Frameset attributes include whether or not to display borders between
pages in the frameset, as well as the width and/or height of various frames
within the frameset. Both attributes are defined in the Property inspector.
The tricky part is selecting the entire frameset to access these features.

The easiest way to select an entire frameset is to view the Frames panel
(Window > Frames). Click on the border that surrounds the entire Frames
panel to select the frameset. The frameset will be selected in both the
Frames panel and in the Document window. You can then easily select a
frame by clicking on it in the Frames panel (**Figure 27a**).

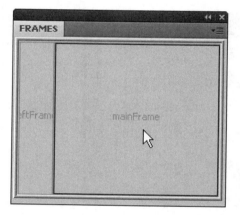

Figure 27a Selecting a frame
using the Frames panel.

Often, framesets are formatted so that there is no visible border
between frames in a browser window. The "page" appears to be a single
page in a browser, even though it is in fact at least three pages.

By default, framesets generated using Dreamweaver's page designs
are formatted to display no border between frames. To add a border to
a selected frame, choose a border color from the Border color swatch.
Then choose Yes from the Borders pop-up menu in the Property inspector (**Figure 27b**).

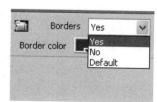

Figure 27b Defining a border for a frame in the
Property inspector.

To define the widths (or heights) of frames within a selected frameset, use the RowCol Selection area in the Property inspector to click a row or column in your frameset. Then choose a value for the selected column or row in the Column Value or Row Value field. Values can be either fixed (in pixels) or a percent. Or, you can make a column width Relative, which means it will fill all space left over after columns with fixed widths are displayed (**Figure 27c**).

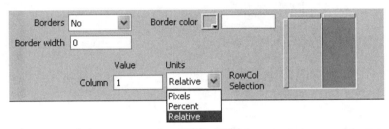

Figure 27c Defining a frame that will fill all available space after fixed-width frames display.

You can define scroll attributes (whether or not to display scroll bars), as well as set resize permission (whether or not to allow a viewer to click and drag on the border between frames and resize them in his or her browser) for frames selected in the Frames panel.

Making Frames More Accessible

As noted in the introduction to this chapter, frames provide an accessibility challenge for vision-impaired visitors. This is because separating content into more than one page can be confusing when that content is read aloud.

Dreamweaver provides a way to define descriptive page titles for each embedded page. Normally, page titles are not relevant for embedded pages. The title of the container page for the frameset displays in the title bar of a browser, and for non-vision-impaired visitors, it all looks like one page.

On the other hand, page titles for each embedded page provide navigation assistance to vision-impaired visitors. If you select the proper accessibility settings, Dreamweaver will prompt you to define page titles for each embedded page

(continued on next page)

(continued)
when you generate a frameset. To enable this feature, choose Edit > Preferences (Windows) or Dreamweaver > Preferences (Mac). Select the Accessibility category in the Preferences dialog, and select the Frames check box. Click OK in the dialog. You'll then be prompted to add page titles to embedded pages in framesets.

Click a specific frame in the Frames panel. The Property inspector then makes settings available for scroll bar display in the Scroll pop-up menu. You can choose Yes (always display a scrollbar), No (never display a scrollbar), Auto (display a scroll bar only as needed), or Default (whatever a browser defaults to). You can enable viewer resizing of frames by deselecting the No resize check box (**Figure 27d**).

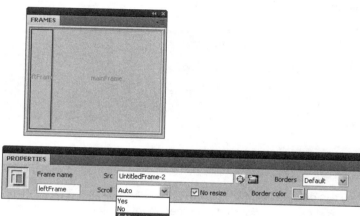

Figure 27d Enabling a scroll bar (only as needed) for a selected frame.

#28 Defining Links Between Frames

Defining links in framesets presents a special challenge. Since technically each frame in a frameset is a *different* HTML page, you need to click on a link in one page and have the link open in a *different* HTML page. And you have to "tell" the link what page to open in. Sounds confusing, but I'll walk you through the whole process here.

For example, let's see how this works in a simple, basic, two-frame frameset with a left navigation frame and a right main frame. Links clicked in the left frame *open in the right frame*. The right side of the frameset changes as new pages open in that frame depending on which link is clicked in the left frame.

This is done by defining a target frame for links. After you define a link for text or an image using the Property inspector (enter the linked page in the Link box), define a target for that link from the Target pop-up menu in the Property inspector.

When you generate a frameset from one of Dreamweaver's frameset page designs, you automatically assign names to each frame within the frameset. These named frames show up in a list when you click the Target pop-up menu in the Property inspector (**Figure 28**).

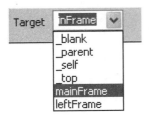

Figure 28 Choosing a target for a link in a frameset.

Be Careful When Assigning Link Targets to Frames

It can be rather disastrous if you don't define the target for a link in a frameset, for example, when a link doesn't open in the appropriate frame but instead opens in the frame from which the link was launched.

Another Good Reason to Rely on Dreamweaver Samples

When you generate framesets using Dreamweaver page designs, each frame is automatically named with a helpful name (like leftFrame or mainFrame). Those frame names are then available in the Target pop-up menu in the Property inspector when you define frame links.

Dreamweaver doesn't do *all* the work for you, however. You still need to remember to define an appropriate frame target for links launched from a frame.

CHAPTER FIVE

Designing Pages with Absolute Placement Objects

Cascading Style Sheets (CSS) have evolved as the most flexible and powerful tool for page layout. Page layout with CSS involves writing CSS code that defines placement objects—think of them as "boxes"—that contain content like text, images, or media. The definition of these placement objects includes their location, their background color, padding within them, spacing around them, and other attributes.

Dreamweaver CS4 provides accessible designer-oriented tools for creating and editing CSS page layout in the form of what Dreamweaver calls Absolute Placement (AP) objects.

In this chapter, you will use only local CSS formatting. External style sheets, which can be used to set up styles for any or all pages in your site, are addressed in Chapter 9, "Working with External Style Sheets."

Should you use tables or CSS for page design? Tables are simpler to learn, and you can feel more confident that your pages will look the way you intend in most desktop browsers.

Note
Page design with tables is covered in Chapter 3, "Creating and Formatting Tables."

On the other hand, current thought on Web site construction is that using CSS makes your content easier to distribute on different platforms and can help you make it accessible to users with disabilities. Reader software, which reads page content out loud to visitors with impaired vision, can interpret CSS layout and present page content in a more coherent way than if blocks of content are laid out in table cells. In Dreamweaver, working with AP objects is more like designing in Adobe Illustrator, Adobe Photoshop, or Adobe InDesign; however, it is somewhat less predictable in its display in a wide range of browsing devices.

#29 Defining AP Objects

AP divs are containers on a Web page that hold content such as type, images, or other objects like media. AP divs are defined by their location on a page and their size (measured in pixels). Dreamweaver allows you to simply draw AP divs on the page, just as if you were designing a page layout in a program like Illustrator or InDesign. As you draw, resize, or move an AP div, Dreamweaver generates CSS code that defines or redefines the location and size of that AP div.

To draw an AP div in an open document, choose Insert > Layout Objects > AP Div. An AP div appears in the document. By default, this AP div is 200 pixels by 115 pixels and is located at the top-left edge of your page (**Figure 29a**).

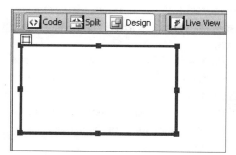

Figure 29a A default AP div in the Document window.

When you generate an AP div, it is selected, and you can edit it. If you deselect the AP div by clicking elsewhere on the page, you can reselect it by clicking on the AP div border.

You can move or relocate an AP div in the Document window. To move an AP div, click the AP div handle (the icon in the upper-left corner of the selected AP div) and simply drag it to another part of the page (**Figure 29b**).

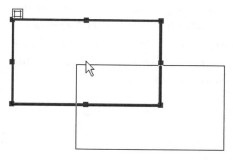

Figure 29b Moving an AP div.

You can also draw an AP div interactively using the Draw AP Div tool in the Layout view of the Insert panel. Choose Window > Insert to display the Draw AP Div tool (**Figure 29c**).

Figure 29c Selecting the Draw AP Div tool from the Insert panel.

When the Draw AP Div tool cursor displays as a crosshair icon, click and draw anywhere on the page to generate an AP div. When you release your mouse cursor, the AP div container is generated.

Dreamweaver offers tools to resize or align multiple AP divs. This is useful, for example, if you want to display several thumbnail images aligned vertically (their tops aligned) on a page. To do this, first Shift-click to select all the AP divs you want to resize or align. Then choose Modify > Arrange. From the submenu, you can select an alignment option (Align Left, Align Right, Align Top [**Figure 29d**], or Align Bottom), or you can select Make Same Width or Make Same Height.

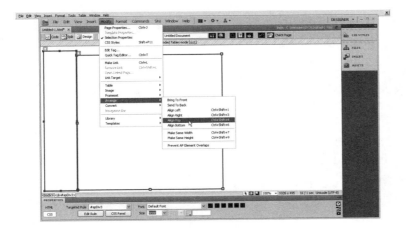

Figure 29d Aligning two AP divs on their top edges.

A Typical Page Layout

You can, of course, generate as many AP divs on a page as you desire. For example, you might create one AP div on the left side of your page as a placeholder for navigation elements, another AP div on the top of your page for a banner, and a third AP div to hold the body of your page content.

CSS, AP, and Compatibility

Display support for AP divs in the Dreamweaver Document window without Live view turned on is uneven. Some AP div features can be previewed in the Document window without Live view but others cannot. To reliably see how AP divs will look in a particular browser, toggle back and forth between Live view on and off or preview the page in that browser. To preview in a browser, choose File > Preview in Browser. If you have more than one installed browser, select the desired browser from the submenu.

Finding Nonvisible AP Divs

Sometimes developers use invisible AP divs as interactive, programmed elements that appear when some action takes place. For example, rolling over an image might cause a nonvisible AP div to change its appearance and become visible. If you assign nonvisible attributes to an AP div, it is often hard to select that AP div in the Document window. AP divs with no visibility do not display in the Document window unless they are selected.

The solution is to select a nonvisible AP div in the AP Elements panel. View the AP Elements panel by choosing Window > AP Elements. In the AP Elements panel, you can select any AP and the outline of the AP div becomes visible in the Document window.

Note

If you use the Modify menu to make selected AP divs the same height or width, the larger AP divs will change size to match the smallest AP div.

You can also embed an AP div within another AP div. This is somewhat similar to embedding a table inside a table.

Note

See #25, "Embedding Tables Within Tables," for a discussion of the pros and cons of that technique.

To embed an AP div within an AP div, click inside one AP div, and then insert another AP div. It's easy to embed one AP div inside another by accident. When you do that, you create unnecessarily complex pages that are difficult to edit. If your CSS page designs are too complex for AP divs, consider invoking definable div tags.

Tip

Div tags are explored in #32, "Defining Div Tags for Page Design."

#**30** Formatting AP Divs in the Property Inspector

You can move and resize AP divs using the Property inspector. Defining location and size in the Property inspector is more precise than clicking and dragging with a mouse because you can define exact location, height, and width to the pixel.

To define a location on a page in the Property inspector for a selected AP div, enter a distance from the left edge of the page (in pixels) in the L (for Left) field, and then enter a distance from the top of the page in the T (for Top) field. An AP div with L and T values of zero will be placed in the upper-left corner of the page (**Figure 30a**).

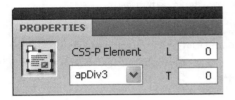

Figure 30a Placing an AP div in the upper-left corner of a page.

Technically, you *can* create overlapping AP divs. You might be able to produce some cutting-edge page designs this way and come close to simulating the freedom you have in programs like Illustrator, Photoshop, or InDesign to stack objects on top of each other.

If you do overlap AP divs, you assign Z-Index values to selected AP divs in the Property inspector to define the AP divs' "front-to-back" properties. AP divs with higher Z-Index values display *on top of* AP divs with lower Z-Index values.

Overlapping AP divs are not universally supported in different browsing environments. They are less reliable than AP divs in general. And, unless you are skilled at CSS, there are a number of pitfalls in designing with overlapping AP divs that can cause your Web page to fall apart and look terrible in browsers. For instance, AP divs often expand in size in different browsing environments in a way that can turn your page into gibberish if overlapping AP divs are used.

Preventing AP Div Overlaps and Converting AP Divs to Tables

Because many designers find that using AP divs is a more intuitive way to design pages than using tables, Dreamweaver allows you to design a page in AP divs. Then if you choose to do so, you can convert the entire page to a table layout, which may display more predictably in various browsers than a CSS-based page. To convert AP divs to tables in the Document window, choose Modify > Convert > AP Divs to Table.

However, if your AP divs overlap, Dreamweaver will not convert them to a table, because tables can't handle overlapping cells. So, if you want to design in AP divs and convert to a table, avoid overlapping AP divs. The AP Elements panel has a Prevent Overlaps check box that will not allow you to place one AP div on top of another.

The other definable elements of AP divs include the following (**Figure 30b**):

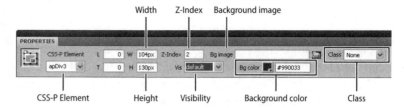

Figure 30b Defining AP div properties in the Property inspector.

- **CSS-P Element:** Defines a name for the AP div for use in scripts or CSS attributes. The name must contain only alphanumeric characters—no spaces—and start with a letter.

- **W:** Width in pixels.

- **H:** Height in pixels.

- **Z-Index:** A numerical value for the bottom-to-top order of an AP div that overlaps others. Higher-value AP divs appear on top of lower-value AP divs.

- **Vis:** Defines visibility. Normally, AP div content is visible, but AP divs used in scripts are sometimes hidden and then made visible later by actions of a visitor.

- **Bg image:** Defines the image that appears as a background in the AP div.

- **Bg color:** Defines the background color for an AP div. If you defined a Bg image, the image will override a background color.

- **Class:** Applies style using a CSS class. See Chapter 6, "Formatting Text," and Chapter 9, "Working with External Style Sheets," for an explanation of how to define CSS classes.

#31 Managing AP Divs in the AP Elements Panel

The AP Elements panel is valuable when you are designing a page with AP divs. You can easily select AP divs in the AP Elements panel (even if you have set the AP divs' visibility to hidden) and make them visible in the Document window.

The AP Elements panel also provides a different and sometimes easier way to define AP div visibility and Z-Index values than using the Property inspector. For example, you can see the properties of many AP divs simultaneously in the AP Elements panel, which comes in handy when you are designing complex interactive pages with AP divs that are either hidden or visible, depending on the state of a script that governs their properties.

You can also rename AP divs in the AP Elements panel, but AP div names must be alphanumeric and cannot start with a number.

View the AP Elements panel by choosing Window > AP Elements. The panel appears with all existing AP divs listed (**Figure 31a**).

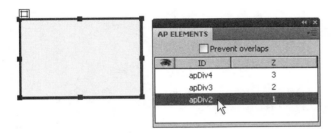

Figure 31a Selecting an AP div in the AP Elements panel.

You select an AP div in the Document window by clicking it in the AP Elements panel. To rename an AP div in the AP Elements panel, double-click the AP div name and enter a new name. You can also switch among the three visibility states in the AP Elements panel by clicking in the visibility column on the left. The closed-eye icon means the AP div is hidden. The open-eye icon means the AP div is visible. No icon signifies default status, which generally means the AP div is visible unless a browser setting conflicts with it (**Figure 31b**).

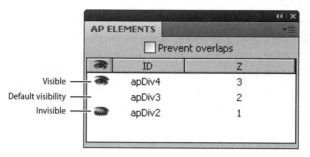

Figure 31b Defining visibility for AP divs.

#**32** Defining Div Tags for Page Design

Dreamweaver AP divs allow designers to lay out pages using familiar tools, and Dreamweaver generates CSS code to match. A somewhat less-intuitive method of generating page layout with CSS in Dreamweaver CS4 is to define div tags. The terminology is confusing: AP div? div tag? The difference is that AP divs are easier to define but do not permit as many formatting options as div tags. Both are generated in the Dreamweaver Document window. Neither AP divs nor div tags require that you learn CSS coding—in both cases Dreamweaver CS4 generates code for you. But while AP divs can be mainly defined and formatted using the Property inspector, more complex and powerful div tags are managed in the CSS panel.

With divs you can define many more attributes than with AP divs. Like AP divs, divs can be positioned at absolute locations on a page, but they can also be positioned *relative* to other locations on a page, or they can *float*—position themselves in relation to other objects on the page. Like AP divs, divs can be sized, but you can also define spacing between them or padding within them, as you can with table cells.

In fact, you can apply an almost unlimited number of attribute combinations to divs, including border color, thickness, and type. And these div attributes are more predictable in different browsing environments.

In Dreamweaver, there are almost as many ways to generate and define a div as there are possible attributes. The following set of steps provides a digestible approach that I use to teach students how to create divs.

To create a div and specify its position:

1. In a new document, select Insert > Layout Objects > Div Tag. The Insert Div Tag dialog appears.

   Note
   The Insert Div Tag dialog does not help to define the positioning, size, or other attributes of the div you want to create. But it does allow you to name it.

2. In the ID field in the Insert Div Tag dialog (**Figure 32a**), enter an alpha-numeric name (start with a letter; spaces are not allowed). Pick a name that will help you identify this object in case you create many divs.

(continued on next page)

Figure 32a Naming a class associated with a div tag.

3. Do not click OK yet. All you've done so far is establish an invisible, size-less section on your page. Instead, click the New CSS Rule button in the Insert Div Tag dialog. The New CSS Rule dialog opens. In the next set of steps, you will define CSS rules that apply to the div you created.

4. In the New CSS Rule dialog, leave the Selector Type at Class, which is the default. Classes are highly flexible and can be applied to any ele-ment (including your div). Select This Document Only from the Rule Definition pop-up menu. The Name field will display the class name you assigned in step 2 (**Figure 32b**).

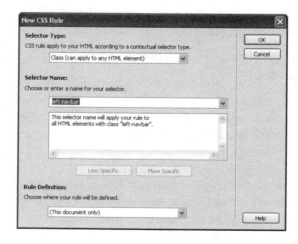

Figure 32b Naming a class with style attributes that will apply to a div.

Designing Pages with Absolute Placement Objects

5. Click OK in the New CSS Rule dialog. The CSS Rule Definition dialog opens. Here is where you set up the class attributes that will be applied to your new div. Click the Positioning category to choose which type of positioning to use when specifying the location of your div, define the div's size, and then define its location on or relative to other parts of the page (**Figure 32c**).

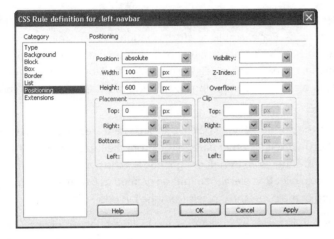

Figure 32c Defining the rules for the CSS class, which will determine the positioning of a div.

6. In the Positioning category in the CSS Rule Definition dialog, choose a positioning type from the Position pop-up menu.

- Choosing Absolute places the object at specific values from the upper-left corner of the page.

- Choosing Fixed freezes the object on a page so that when a visitor scrolls up or down, the object stays in the same place.

- Choosing Relative places the object relative to its position in the text flow of the page. If your cursor is at the top of a Web page, absolute and relative positioning have the same effect, but if your cursor is in the middle of some text, relative positioning places the object a defined distance to the left of and below the current cursor point.

(continued on next page)

External vs Document Styles

If you select the top Define In option instead of the This Document Only option, you must create a new, external style sheet file. External style sheets are explained in Chapter 9.

Tip
Choosing Relative positioning without any offsets is often a way to give a div a needed "hasLayout" property that Internet Explorer versions earlier than version 7 require to display some layouts properly.

- Choosing Static places the div container at its location in the text flow.

7. Define the width and height of your div container in the Width and Height fields. For example, a left navigation element might have a width of 100 pixels. Choose a unit of measurement from the pop-up menu next to each box (pixels are normally used for defining dimensions in Web design, and using pixels is the most reliable way to size objects).

8. Define the position of your box in the Placement area. You can define location in pixels (or other units) either from the top or bottom of the page and either from the left or right edge of the page. For instance, a left-side navigation element might be defined as 0 (zero) pixels from the top of the page and 0 pixels from the left edge of the page.

9. The four Clip boxes work like masking in illustration programs. Clipping hides part of the outside of the content of a CSS positioning object. Leave these check boxes deselected; usually, you will not want to clip content.

10. Visibility defines whether or not the div is visible. Unless you are designing div tags for a JavaScript application, leave the default setting at visible.

11. The Z-Index box defines how the div will move in front of or behind other objects. Positioning objects with higher Z-Index values appear on top of objects with lower Z-Index values. If your positioning objects do not overlap, Z-Index values are irrelevant, so you do not need to enter any value in the Z-Index boxes.

12. The Overflow pop-up menu defines how text that does not fit in the positioning object will appear in a browser. The Visible option displays all content, even if it doesn't fit in the div. The Hidden option hides all content that does not fit in the div. The Scroll option displays a scroll bar, so the div looks like a miniature browser window with its

own scroll bar(s). And the Auto option leaves div display up to the user's browsing environment, so leave the Overflow display at Auto.

13. Once you have defined the options in the Positioning category, you have defined the basic location and size of your object (div). Use the Border category to apply borders to your object. Use the Box category to define buffer spacing between content and the box (Padding) or spacing between objects (Margin). Spacing is usually unnecessary with divs, but allowing 6 pixels of padding is often a good way to keep the content of different divs from bumping into each other.

14. When you are finished defining options for your div, click OK. You can enter content in your positioned div by clicking inside it and typing or by inserting images (**Figure 32d**).

Figure 32d Inserting content into a positioned div.

#**33** Editing Layout Div Tags in the CSS Styles Panel

You can edit layout div tags in the CSS Styles dialog the same way you learned to define a div tag in #32, "Defining Div Tags for Page Design." To do that, select the CSS tag in the CSS Styles panel, and choose Edit from the panel menu (**Figure 33a**). The CSS Styles panel reopens, and you can change any of your existing parameters.

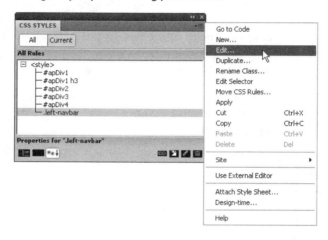

Figure 33a
Editing a
CSS div tag.

But there is an easier way to make quick, interactive adjustments to the parameters of a CSS div tag used as a positioning box. When you select the tag in the CSS Styles panel, the defined parameters for the selected CSS style display in a handy table at the bottom of the CSS Styles panel. Each parameter is editable within the CSS Styles panel: Just enter or select a new value for any displayed parameter (**Figure 33b**).

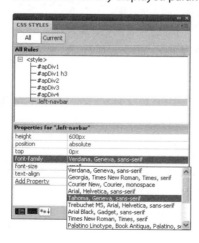

Figure 33b Editing a CSS div tag in the CSS Styles panel.

#34 Using Rulers, Guides, and Grids

Since AP divs and div tags allow you to design pages in an intuitive, interactive, graphical environment, wouldn't it be nice if you could use design features like rulers, guides, and gridlines to make it easy to align and place layout objects? Well, the good news is you can!

Dreamweaver CS4's rulers, guides, and gridlines display much like those in Illustrator, InDesign, and Photoshop. Combined with AP divs and definable div tags, they allow Dreamweaver's Document window to function as a graphical design workspace.

To display rulers in an open document, choose View > Rulers > Show. The Rulers submenu also allows you to choose pixels, inches, or centimeters (**Figure 34a**).

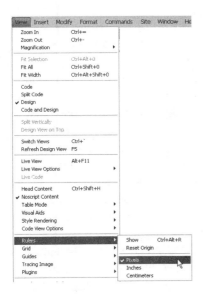

Figure 34a Choosing a unit of measurement for rulers.

You can even redefine the horizontal and/or vertical zero points for the rulers. Do this by dragging the icon at the intersection of the horizontal and vertical rulers into the Document window. The point at which you release your mouse becomes the new zero point for the horizontal and vertical rulers (**Figure 34b**). To reset the rulers' zero points, choose View > Rulers > Reset Origin.

Rulers, Guides, and Grids Are for Design Purposes Only

Rulers, guides, and grids do not actually become part of your Web page. They appear in the Document window (in Design view only) to help you place or align objects.

Rulers, guides, and grids make it easy to place many AP divs or defined div tags on your page, size them, and align them.

Regardless of which ruler, guide, or grid display you select in Dreamweaver, these elements *do not* display in a browser window

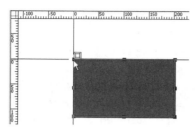

Figure 34b Setting a customized horizontal and vertical zero point for rulers to the top left of an AP div.

To place a horizontal or vertical guide on the page, click and drag a ruler into the Document window (**Figure 34c**).

Figure 34c Placing a horizontal guide on top of an AP div.

To edit the location of a guide, click and drag it. You can also double-click a guide to edit the guide location or unit of measurement.

Guides can be locked to prevent accidental editing: Choose View > Guides > Lock Guides. Guides can also be made "magnetic" so that they either snap to objects on the page or objects on the page snap to them. To make a guide snap to elements on the page, choose View > Guides > Guides Snap to Elements. To make elements snap to guides, choose View > Guides > Snap to Guides. Clear guides by choosing View > Guides > Clear Guides.

Grids can be displayed by choosing View > Grid > Show Grid. Make grids magnetic by choosing View > Grid > Snap to Grid.

Define grid properties by choosing View > Grid > Grid Settings. The Grid Settings dialog allows you to change the color of gridlines, spacing between grids, grid display and snap properties, and display (dots or lines). Click Apply to preview changes to the grid, or click OK to close the dialog and change grid settings in the Document window (**Figure 34d**).

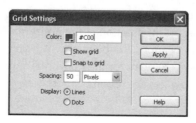

Figure 34d Editing grid display settings.

Designing Pages with Absolute Placement Objects

CHAPTER SIX

Formatting Text

The Property inspector in Dreamweaver CS4 has been revamped to reflect two basic options for formatting text. You can apply text formatting *either* by using HTML tags *or* by generating on-the-spot CSS (Cascading Style Sheet) styles.

HTML formatting uses HTML attributes—modifiers attached to a relatively primitive set of HTML formatting tags—to apply formatting to text. HTML formatting is restricted to only a few formatting options: You can apply an HTML tag (for example, Paragraph Text or six levels of headings). You can assign boldface or italics to text. You can apply bullet or numbered list formatting. And you can indent or outdent text.

The advantages? HTML formatting is universally supported in every browsing environment and is less confusing to apply than CSS formatting. The disadvantage? HTML text formatting is very limited.

CSS formatting opens up the potential for much more freedom to format text. Using the Property inspector to apply CSS formatting automatically generates a new CSS style for the specific set of attributes you apply to text. For example, if you define a block of text with red, 12 point, italic, Arial formatting, that set of formatting attributes is automatically saved as a CSS style.

The advantage to using CSS for text formatting is that it provides for much more flexibility and many more formatting options. One disadvantage, or perhaps better put one challenge, is to control the number of CSS styles that are generated so as to not create page files that are choking with CSS code that increases file size and makes it confusing to edit page layout and text formatting.

The how-tos in this chapter will explain more about these options in detail and walk you through using both approaches to format text.

#35 Apply HTML Tags to Text

The most basic and foundational way you apply formatting to text in HTML is by assigning *already defined* tags. HTML tags are basic because they provide a minimalist set of format attributes (mainly type size and emphasis) and foundational because HTML tags can be *enhanced* by associating CSS rules that enable all kinds of additional text formatting attributes.

HTML tags are interpreted in standard ways by browsers. For example, h1 tags (short for Heading 1) are larger than h2 tags, which are larger than h3 tags, and so on down to h6 tags (typically used for "fine print" on pages). In addition to the six heading tags, the Paragraph tag is normally applied to most page text.

An effective text formatting technique is to *first* assign HTML tags to all text on your page. *Then* you can define CSS attributes for those tags, redefining and customizing how the Paragraph tag and the Heading tags display.

Among the advantages to this technique is that it makes it possible for visitors in various browsing environments to either strip out or adjust the CSS formatting you define as necessary. A mobile device, for example, might by default display all Paragraph Text in a font and size easily viewed on that device. Or a sight-impaired visitor might set up his or her browsing environment to display HTML tags in accessible ways.

To apply one of the six heading tags or the Paragraph tag to a selected paragraph, first make sure you have selected the HTML button on the far left of the Property inspector, not the CSS button. This enables HTML options. Then select the text and choose the tag from the Format pop-up menu in the Property inspector (**Figure 35**).

HTML Styles— Similar to Word Processor Styles

The six HTML heading styles, h1 (Heading 1) to h6 (Heading 6), are similar to heading styles used in programs like Adobe InDesign, QuarkXPress, or even Microsoft Word.

Formatting for the Visually Impaired

Adobe Magazine estimates that by 2010, 20 million people in the United States will fall into the category of "sight impaired," which includes strong nearsightedness and color blindness. Relying on HTML tags for font formatting makes it easier for people with vision problems to access your Web pages. By contrast, for example, relying on font colors assigned via CSS for text formatting and to convey content makes that content inaccessible to the color blind. (See "Access Ability: The art, science, and benefits of designing accessible Web sites" by Maxine Williams, *Adobe Magazine*, Summer 1999).

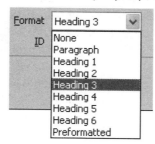

Figure 35 Applying a Heading 3 tag from the Format pop-up menu in the Property inspector.

HTML Tags Are Applied to Paragraphs

You cannot apply an HTML tag, like Paragraph or Heading 1, to selected text only. Paragraph tags and all Heading tags are applied to *entire* paragraphs. To format only selected text, use CSS formatting.

#**36** Format Text with HTML Attributes

In addition to assigning tags to text, you can apply HTML *attributes* to selected text. These HTML attributes are very limited to formatting features like boldface, italics, and font color. Applying attributes like font size, type, and color with HTML is being phased out as a supported text formatting technique. And as of Dreamweaver CS4, this option is no longer available from the Property inspector.

However, limited HTML text formatting attributes—Bold, Italic, Text Outdent, Text Indent, Bullet Lists, and Automatic Numbering—are still supported and available from the Property inspector.

You can apply HTML attributes to selected text in the Property inspector by clicking the Bold, Italic, Unordered List (bullet points), Ordered List (automatic numbering), Text Outdent, or Text Indent buttons (**Figure 36a**).

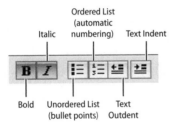

Figure 36a HTML text formatting attributes in the Property inspector.

If you apply an HTML tag *and* an HTML formatting attribute to text, the attribute will override the formatting applied by the tag. So, for example, if you apply the Paragraph tag to an entire paragraph, you can still apply specific attributes (like boldface) to selected text (**Figure 36b**).

Figure 36b Applying boldface to selected text.

#37 Format HTML Tags with CSS Attributes

You can use CSS to customize the way Heading styles and the Paragraph style appear on your Web page. Such customized Paragraph and Heading styles provide uniform text formatting, either on a page or, when the styles are defined in an external style sheet, throughout your site.

To define custom CSS formatting for an HTML Heading tag or for the Paragraph tag, follow these steps:

1. Choose Window > CSS Styles to display the CSS Styles panel.

2. From the CSS Styles panel menu, choose New (**Figure 37a**).

Figure 37a Defining a new CSS style in the CSS Styles panel.

3. The New CSS Rule dialog opens. Choose Tag from the Selector Type pop-up menu (**Figure 37b**).

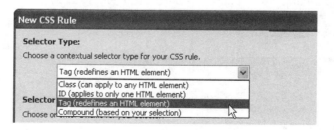

Figure 37b Choosing the HTML Tag category as the target of the CSS format.

4. From the Selector Name pop-up menu, choose one of the six heading styles (H1, H2, H3, H4, H5, or H6) or the Paragraph style (P) and click OK (**Figure 37c**). The CSS Rule Definition dialog opens.

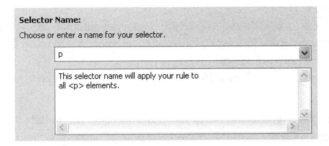

Figure 37c Selecting the Paragraph tag to redefine with custom CSS.

Once you open the CSS Rule Definition dialog for your selected HTML tag, you can define CSS formatting the way you would with any text. For an explanation of how to do that, see #39, "Define and Apply CSS Rules."

#**38** Create Class CSS Formatting Rules for Text

Class styles are independent of HTML tags. When you assign formatting to selected text using a *Custom* or *Class* style, you can apply that formatting to *any* selected text. In this way, Class styles are different than CSS rules associated with an HTML tag, which can only be applied to entire paragraphs (in general).

Dreamweaver CS4 forces you to create Class styles automatically when you attempt to apply formatting like font style, color, or size using CSS mode in the Property inspector.

To define CSS text formatting rules for a Class style, follow these steps:

1. In the Property inspector, click the CSS button on the far left. This enables CSS features of the Property inspector for the selected text (**Figure 38a**).

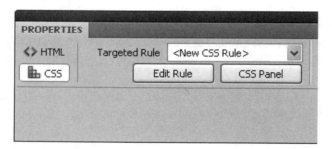

Figure 38a Selecting the CSS category in the Property inspector.

2. Choose New CSS Rule from the Targeted Rule pop-up menu in the Property inspector (**Figure 38b**). Then click the Edit Rule button.

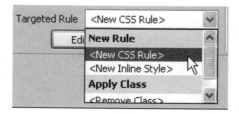

Figure 38b Selecting a New CSS rule in the Property inspector.

3. The New CSS Rule dialog opens. Choose Class from the Selector Type pop-up menu (**Figure 38c**).

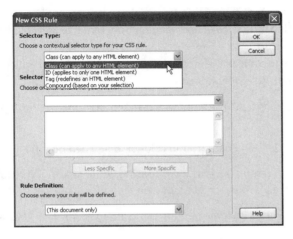

Figure 38c Choosing Class as the type of style.

4. Enter a Class style name in the Selector Name pop-up menu in the New CSS Rule dialog.

Once you open the CSS Rule Definition dialog for your selected Class tag, you can define CSS formatting the way you would with any text. For an explanation of how to do that, see #39, "Define and Apply CSS Rules."

About Class Style Names

Class style names start with an optional period ("."). No spaces are allowed, nor any punctuation (except for the optional initial period).

#39 Define and Apply CSS Rules

Whether you are defining CSS rules for an HTML tag (see #37, "Format HTML Tags with CSS Attributes") or for a Class tag (see #38, "Create Class CSS Formatting Rules for Text), once you choose a tag or name your Class style, the CSS Rule Definition dialog opens. Here you can apply a wide range of formatting attributes to text, ranging from font size and color to word and line spacing.

The following are some of the more useful formatting category options available in the CSS Rule Definition dialog:

- **Type:** Defines font, size, weight, style (italic or roman), and line height.

- **Background:** Defines a background color or image behind type.

- **Block:** Defines features such as word spacing, letter spacing, vertical and horizontal alignment, and indentation.

- **Box:** Defines width, height, padding, and margins for CSS layout elements.

- **Border:** Defines the style, thickness, and color of borders around text.

- **List:** Defines the type of bullet or numbering.

- **Positioning:** Defines positioning of CSS layout elements.

- **Extensions:** Defines page breaks, cursor display (when a cursor is moved over selected text), and special effects like blur or inversion.

The Type category in the CSS Rule Definition dialog is where most basic text formatting rules are defined for a style (**Figure 39a**).

Font-family: Choose a preferred font and alternate fonts

Color: The palette presents the 216 Web-safe colors

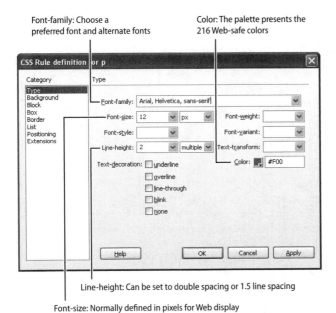

Line-height: Can be set to double spacing or 1.5 line spacing

Font-size: Normally defined in pixels for Web display

Figure 39a The Type category showing Arial font, 12 pixel font size, red color, and double-spacing selected.

From the Font-family pop-up menu, choose a set of fonts. Font display requires that a viewer have the appropriate font installed on his or her computer, so alternate fonts are listed in case the preferred font is not supported.

From the Font-size pop-up menu, you can define font size either in units (like pixels or points) or in relative sizes (like small, medium, or large).

Applying Font Colors

The 216 or so set of what used to be called "Web-safe colors" has gone in, out, and back into style. Modern computers support far more than the 256 colors that were the basis for the "Web-safe" palette (some colors were reserved for the operating system). However, with the proliferation of mobile device Web browsing, there is again a value in constraining your choices of Web colors to the 216 color palette that appears when you click the color swatch in the CSS Rule Definition dialog.

Generally speaking, defining font sizes in pixels is the most effective way to control font size on a computer screen (**Figure 39b**).

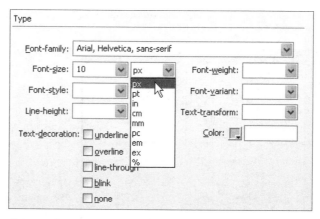

Figure 39b Assigning a 10 pixel font size to a style.

You can define italics using the Font-style pop-up menu and boldface from the Font-weight pop-up menu.

Line spacing is an underrated and accessible way to create a unique and readable look for large blocks of text. For example, you assign 1 ½ line spacing (midway between single spacing and double spacing between lines) by entering 150 in the Line-height box and choosing % from the accompanying pop-up menu (**Figure 39c**). Selecting 1.5 as the value and Multiple from the accompanying pop-up menu accomplishes the same thing.

Figure 39c Assigning 1.5 line spacing.

The Color swatch in the Type category of the CSS Rule Definition dialog allows you to choose font color, either interactively from a panel or by entering a hexadecimal (six digit) code for a color.

Of the set of Text-decoration check boxes, the most widely used is the None check box, and it is mostly used to deselect underlining from text styles used in links (normally, links display as underlined text, but clicking the None check box when defining a link style disables the underlining).

After you define all font characteristics for a style, click OK to save the style definition.

To apply a style to selected text, choose the style from the Targeted Rule pop-up menu in the Property inspector (**Figure 39d**).

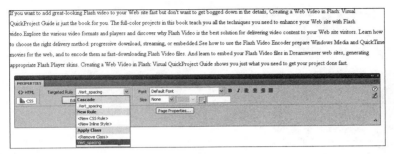

Figure 39d Choosing a CSS style for selected text; here the style applies 1.5 multiple line spacing.

#40 Edit CSS Rules

Tabs in the CSS Styles Panel

With the All tab selected at the top of the CSS styles panel, you see a list of styles. You may need to click the Expand icon to the left of <style> to reveal the styles to edit. If the Current tab is selected at the top of the CSS Styles panel, you can see the attributes of a CSS style by clicking on text to which the style has been assigned.

There are two accessible ways to edit existing CSS styles. One is to select the style in the CSS Styles panel, and then click the Edit Rule button (**Figure 40a**). This reopens the CSS Rule Definition dialog in which you can change any of the existing rules for the style.

Figure 40a Opening the CSS Rule Definition dialog from the CSS Styles panel.

Edit Rule button

Another even more accessible technique is to edit or add CSS style rules right in the CSS panel without having to open the CSS Rule Definition dialog. You can change the attribute of any defined CSS style rule by clicking on the property in the bottom half of the CSS Styles panel and choosing new values from pop-up menus within the CSS Styles panel (**Figure 40b**).

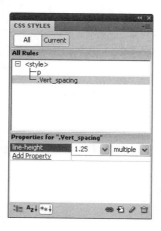

Figure 40b Changing line spacing for a selected style in the CSS Styles panel.

Formatting Text

And, you can use the Add Property hyperlink in the bottom half of the CSS Styles panel to open a pop-up menu that displays dozens of definable style rules, many of which are applicable to text (**Figure 40c**).

Figure 40c Adding a color rule to a CSS style definition.

CHAPTER SEVEN

Working with Images

"Web-compatible image" used to mean just a JPEG, a GIF, or a PNG format file. Well, actually, it still does mean that. Only those three formats are universally supported in Web browsers (formats like TIFF, Adobe Illustrator's AI format, and Photoshop's native PSD format are *not* supported in Web browsers).

However, Dreamweaver CS4 makes it easy to embed an image onto a Web page from just about any source, and then convert it to one of the three supported Web image formats.

And, Dreamweaver CS4 includes some very basic image-editing tools so you can crop or adjust contrast in a photo right in Dreamweaver.

That said, you'll still need to prepare images in advance (in another program) before you place them on a Web page. Dreamweaver's very limited photo-editing features aren't in the same ballpark as those in Photoshop or even the free software that comes with digital cameras. In addition, Dreamweaver does not provide drawing tools to create illustrations—for that you still need Adobe Illustrator.

So, you'll start this chapter by exploring the process of preparing images for the Web in *other* programs. You'll then learn how to use Dreamweaver to place the image, align text to flow around the image, and assign links to either the entire image or part of the image (an image map).

#**41** Preparing Images for the Web

Web browsers recognize three types of image formats: JPEG, GIF, and PNG. The first step in preparing images for the Web is to save or export them to one of these formats.

You can either save the images you create using Adobe Illustrator, Adobe Photoshop, or other programs as GIFs, JPEGs or PNGs, *or* you can directly open a Photoshop file in the Dreamweaver Document window or paste any image from any source using your operating clipboard.

This process launches Dreamweaver's Image Preview window, where you can convert the opened or pasted Photoshop file to a JPEG, GIF, or PNG.

In general, the JPEG format is much better for photos; it supports a more complex set of colors than GIF or PNG. The advantage to using GIF and PNG formats is the ability to have a *transparent*, or invisible, background that allows the Web page background to show through. This creates the impression that the image is sitting directly on the page. The ability to make a color (usually the background color) invisible makes GIF or PNG the preferred format for icons and other graphics that show the page background "through" the image (**Figure 41a**).

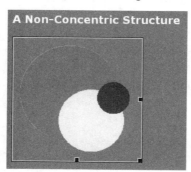

Figure 41a A GIF image with a transparent color allows the (gray) page background to show through.

Can you get away with simply using a JPEG image file straight from your digital camera in a Web site? Maybe, but the file probably won't work well, even though the JPEG format available as an option in your digital camera is Web compatible. The file will likely be too large in dimensions and file size, and will likely be formatted for print, not Web display.

To prepare a file for the Web, you'll want to choose appropriate color, size, and resolution settings. Web images are generally saved at 72 dots per inch (dpi). This is much *lower* than print resolution (which is normally set to at least 300 dpi) because monitor resolution is 72 dpi on Macs and 96 dpi in Windows.

Which Web-compatible Format Is Best?

GIF and PNG images have the advantage of allowing you to make one color transparent. This feature is usually used to make the image background transparent. GIF images can be animated (a set of GIFs is stored in a single GIF to simulate animation). PNG images can be of higher image quality and have more nuanced color representation than GIF images.

JPEG images are the standard format for photos. JPEG images are compressed, which reduces file size and allows them to open more quickly in a Web page. They also include sophisticated color accuracy. JPEG images can vary widely in quality, ranging from very small files that reduce colors rather crudely to high-quality images that are much larger in file size.

When you create images for a Web page, you generally try to keep file size small. File size is not much of an issue for print documents; nobody has to sit and stare at a printed book or newspaper waiting for an illustration to download. In contrast, several 5 MB images on a Web page will take quite some time to download over a dial-up connection.

There are two ways to reduce file size: You can make the image smaller, or you can use *compression*. Smaller images are also smaller files, and they download quickly. Many Web sites use *thumbnail* images—small preview versions of a full-sized image. Visitors who want to see a full-sized version of the image, either on the same Web page or on a separate page, can click the thumbnail.

Thumbnail images address two challenges in Web design. They reduce the time it takes to download a page (compared to downloading full-sized images), and they help solve the problem of limited space on the page. It's generally a bad idea to place images on a page that won't fit in a standard-size browser window—roughly 800 pixels (8 inches) wide and 600 pixels (6 inches) high. Providing a set of clickable thumbnails that open full-sized images is a universally applicable technique for presenting images on Web pages (**Figure 41b**).

Figure 41b Visitors at Bruce Hopkins's Web site can click a thumbnail of an image to display the full-sized version.

Progressive Downloading and Interlacing for Web Images

Progressive downloading (for JPEG images) and interlacing downloading (for GIFs) allows images to "fade in" when they download into a browser instead of appearing line by line. These options are available in the preview window for selected GIF or JPEG conversions and are generally a more pleasant way to display large images as they download into a viewing environment.

Compressing Photos for the Web

Compression can drastically reduce file size, speeding up download time. But compression also reduces quality by eliminating nuance in an image. The Save for Web window, available in Adobe products such as Photoshop, Photoshop Elements, and Illustrator, allows you to preview images with different levels of compression and compare them.

Tips for Preparing Images for the Web

- Save the file to JPEG, GIF, or PNG format.

- Create a thumbnail version of the image that is only about 100 pixels wide. The thumbnail will serve as a clickable link to open a larger version of the image.

- Reduce the image to a size that will fit into most browser windows. A useful guide is to keep images smaller than 760 pixels wide by 600 pixels high.

- Experiment with compression using the Save for Web feature available in Photoshop, Photoshop Elements, and Illustrator.

Compression is a technique that reduces the number of pixels that need to be "kept track of" in an image file. This is done by defining only necessary pixels. So, for example, instead of "remembering" that there are 50 contiguous white dots in a photo, a compressed image file will define just one of these pixels and compress the file by simply noting that the other 49 pixels are identical to the defined pixel.

The final step in the process of preparing an image for the Web is to save the image file to the folder on your computer that you use for your Dreamweaver Web site. When you do this, it will be easy to find the image as you use it on your Web page.

#**42** Embedding Images in a Web Page

When an image is ready for the Web, you can embed it in a page in Dreamweaver. Why use the term *embed*? Because the image file remains a distinct file. To your Web site visitors it appears that the image is "part of the page." But in reality a *separate* image file is displayed on your Web page using parameters you define in Dreamweaver that govern the location, size, and other elements of the image.

Start the process of embedding an image by clicking at the beginning of the paragraph of text with which the image will be associated.

With your cursor at the insertion point, choose Insert > Image. The Select Image Source dialog opens. Navigate to the image you want to place on the page, and click Choose (**Figure 42**).

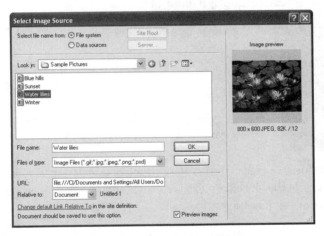

Figure 42 Choosing an image to embed in a Web page.

If the image file you selected is not in the folder you defined as your Dreamweaver site folder, Dreamweaver helpfully offers to save a copy of the image in your site folder. Click Yes in the dialog that appears to avail yourself of this service.

Don't Embed Images in the Middle of a Paragraph

Even if you want to display an image to the right of a line of text, embed the image at the *beginning* of the paragraph. Do this by placing the insertion cursor at the very beginning of the paragraph before choosing Insert > Image.

This might seem counterintuitive, particularly if you're used to laying out images and text in a program like Adobe InDesign or Illustrator. But as you'll learn in #45, "Aligning Text and Images," the relationship of an image to a paragraph is a product of how the image is aligned, not of where it is inserted. Placing an image in the middle or at the end of a paragraph will make image and text alignment harder to control.

#43 Defining Alt Tags for Images

There are many reasons why visitors won't be able to or won't want to see images in their browser. Visitors who rely on screen reader software to read your Web site content aloud will not see your images, nor will visitors using browsers on devices that do not display images. Other visitors to your site might have low-bandwidth connections and elect not to display images.

An Alt tag is code that is displayed if its associated image does not display in a browser window. In addition, with Microsoft Internet Explorer and some other browsers, Alt tag text displays when you roll over an image with the cursor.

Well-designed Web pages provide Alt tags that display when, for any reason, an image does not display (**Figure 43a**).

How Many People Rely on Alt Tags?

Accessibility experts estimate that as many as 30 percent of all Web visitors rely on Alt tags. Visitors with various vision limitations use Alt tags to either replace or supplement what they can (or cannot) see. For instance, many color-blind visitors rely on Alt tags to supplement what they can see in an image. Additionally, many devices such as cell phones and other handheld devices don't display images.

Figure 43a By including an Alt tag, the Web designer ensures that alternate text displays when the image does not.

You can define an Alt tag in the Property inspector by entering text for a selected image in the Alt field. Enter a brief description that will serve as an alternative for visitors who will not see the image (**Figure 43b**).

Alt tag field

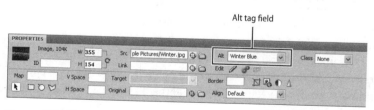

Figure 43b Alt tag text.

Alt tags are more useful if they are not too long; thus, the recommended maximum length is 50 characters. Sometimes that's not enough. For example, if you need to convey information depicted in a graph, map, or detailed photo, you might want to provide more information to visitors than fits in an Alt tag.

The solution is to provide a separate file that contains unlimited text. This file is accessed by the long description (longdesc) attribute. The content of a longdesc attribute is not text; it is the name of a Web page that contains a text description. The first step in providing a long description for an image is to create a separate all-text HTML file that describes the image.

After you have created an HTML page with a long description for an image, access the longdesc attribute for a selected image by choosing the Tag inspector (choose Window > Tag Inspector). Expand the CSS/Accessibility category in the Tag panel and use the Browse icon to navigate to the file you created with the long description.

#**44** Editing Images in Dreamweaver

The Downside of Resizing

There are significant drawbacks to both enlarging and shrinking image dimensions in Dreamweaver. If you make an image larger, you will significantly degrade the quality of the image because there is not enough data saved in the image file to display more pixels. As a result, the image will appear grainy, blurry, or raggedy. You will not lose quality in the same way if you make an image smaller. The image file will have enough data to display a smaller version of the image. However, the image quality will often still degrade because Dreamweaver's resizing tools are not sophisticated enough to figure out how to properly eliminate some of the image data. Programs like Photoshop and Photoshop Elements have resampling features that intelligently add or remove pixels as you resize an image. In short, it's best if you can size your image before you bring it into Dreamweaver.

Dreamweaver's limited set of image-editing tools allows you to crop, resample, change brightness and contrast, apply sharpening, and resize an image. When you select an image, Dreamweaver's image-editing tools will display in the Property inspector (**Figure 44a**).

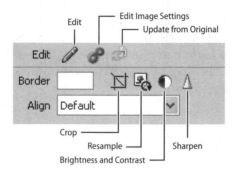

Figure 44a Image-editing tools in the Property inspector.

Note
The Property inspector needs to be expanded to see the Sharpen tool.

The Edit tool launches your system's default image-editing software. The Edit Image Settings tool opens Dreamweaver's Image Preview dialog. Here, you can change the image format (to JPEG, GIF, or PNG), apply smoothing, and tweak other image format settings that vary depending on the image file format selected (**Figure 44b**).

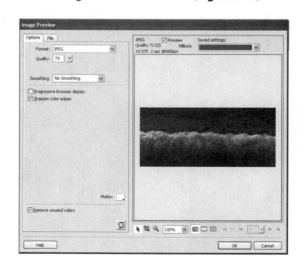

Figure 44b Editing image settings—here, JPEG is the selected file format.

You can resize a selected image by clicking and dragging either the horizontal or vertical sizing handles on the image, or by clicking and dragging the corner handle. Holding down the Shift key as you resize using the corner handle maintains the original height-to-width ratio of the image. The new width and height are indicated in the W and H fields in the Property inspector.

After you exit Image Preview, you can resize an image in the Design window (**Figure 44c**).

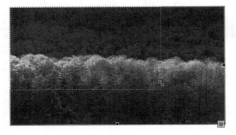

Figure 44c Resizing an image: Hold down the Shift key to maintain the existing height-to-width ratio.

You can also enter width and height dimensions in the W and H fields. When you resize an image in Dreamweaver, the width and height display in boldface type in the Property inspector, and you can use the Reset Image to Original Size icon to revert to the original size.

To trim an image, you can use the Crop tool, which works like a Crop tool in programs like Photoshop. The Resample tool reduces file size after you make an image smaller in Dreamweaver. Until you resample, the image displays in smaller dimensions on the Web page, but the file is not smaller. This means that the resized image will take the same amount of time to download that it did before it was resized. You can reduce file size and eliminate unnecessary pixels by clicking the Resample icon in the Property inspector. The Brightness and Contrast tool and the Sharpen tool, when selected, will open dialogs with very simple sliders that adjust how an image looks.

Editing Photoshop Files

If you place a Photoshop (PSD) file in Dreamweaver, that image will be converted into a Web-accessible format for display. However, if you edit that image using the Edit tool in the Property inspector, the Photoshop file will reopen for editing in Photoshop (assuming you have Photoshop installed on your computer—if not, another default image editor for PSD files will open if you have one installed). For more information about placing Photoshop files in Dreamweaver, see #47, "Placing Photoshop Files in Web Pages."

To open the Brightness/Contrast dialog for a selected image, click the Brightness and Contrast icon in the Property inspector. Select the Preview check box to see the effect of the changes you made to the brightness and/or contrast (**Figure 44d**).

Figure 44d Previewing brightness and contrast changes.

Similarly, the Sharpen dialog has a Preview check box so you can see the effect of the changes you made to sharpen the image (**Figure 44e**).

Figure 44e Previewing changes with adjustments using the Sharpen slider.

Thumbnails are valuable tools for presenting images on a Web page. They take very little space and download quickly, allowing visitors to preview a full-sized image by clicking the thumbnail. Dreamweaver CS4's utility for generating thumbnails requires Fireworks (a trial version can be downloaded from Adobe). The utility that generates thumbnails is actually designed to create a Web photo album (a slide show), but you can use this tool to create thumbnail images from a folder of images. To create thumbnails, follow these steps:

1. In the Document window, choose Commands > Create Web Photo Album (it is not necessary to have a particular page open to do this). The Create Web Photo Album dialog appears. Unless you are generating a Web photo album, you can skip the first three fields in the dialog.

In the Source images folder field, navigate to and select the folder that contains copies of all your full-sized images.

2. In the Destination folder field, navigate to and select the folder in which the generated thumbnails will be saved.

3. In the Thumbnail size field, choose a size (100 x 100 pixels is standard).

4. In the Photo format pop-up menu, choose a quality for the thumbnails. There are two usable options here: JPEG—smaller file creates fast-loading but poor-quality images and JPEG—better quality creates thumbnails with more accurate color but somewhat larger files and longer download time. If high-quality thumbnails are important to conveying your content, choose JPEG—better quality.

5. The other two options in this dialog (GIF webSnap 128 and GIF webSnap 256) are only relevant if you are creating a Web photo album. You can click OK, and then kick back and relax while Dreamweaver (and Fireworks) creates a set of thumbnails.

#45 Aligning Text and Images

A flexible, reliable technique for combining images and text is to align an image either right or left. Aligning an image will flow text to the right (for a left-aligned image) or to the left (for a right-aligned image) of the image (**Figure 45a**).

At the royal court, Hermione plays with Mamillius when Leontes enters, hearing that Camillo has left with Polixenes. Leontes wrongly determines that Camillo had been working for Polixenes for a long time, then accuses Hermione of being unfaithful and sends her to prison, although she publicly denies all. Antigonus and other lords try in vain to change Leontes' mind. He tells them he has sent a messenger to the oracles Delphos and Apollo to confirm or deny his suspicions. At the prison, Antigonus' wife Paulina comes to visit Hermione, but the jailer only lets her see Hermione's lady Emilia. Emilia tells her the stress has caused Hermione to go into labor and have a baby girl. Paulina convinces Hermione to let her bring the baby to Leontes in hopes of calming him. In Leontes' chamber, he muses how he can only take out his revenge on the queen, but not on Polixenes who is too far away. We also learn Prince Mamillius has fallen sick over depression for losing his mother. Paulina arrives and presents Leontes' daughter to him. Leontes denies the child, but Paulina yells at him and insists it is his baby and not Polixenes'. Yet, he still yells at her and then accuses Antigonus of setting his wife up to her outbursts. Leontes then orders Antigonus to burn and kill the baby he calls a bastard. The lords convince him to let the baby live, but Leontes then orders Antigonus to abandon the child in a desert place and let it fiend for itself.

Figure 45a Left-aligned image.

You can also define a horizontal and vertical buffer space between images and the text that flows around them.

Aligned images are associated with a paragraph of text. They are not locked in place on the page but instead move up or down on the page with the paragraph, depending on the size of the visitor's browser window.

To align a selected image, click the Align field in the Property inspector and choose Left or Right from the pop-up menu (**Figure 45b**).

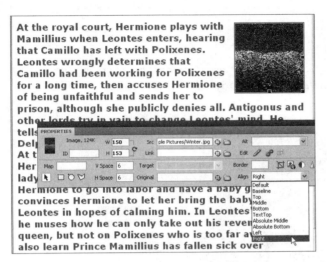

Figure 45b Right-aligning an image in the Property inspector.

When you align images in relation to paragraph text, you almost always want to define horizontal and vertical spacing to separate the edge of the image from the text. If you don't define horizontal and vertical spacing around the image, the image will bump into the text characters (**Figure 45c**).

Figure 45c An image with no horizontal spacing bumps into the paragraph text.

Other Alignment Options

You might notice other alignment options in the Align pop-up menu aside from Left and Right. These options are used to align tiny images that are supposed to appear in a line of text. The ability to do this is, in large part, a holdover from an era when operating systems did not support much in the way of symbols, and it was necessary to provide a way to embed and align tiny images within lines of text. Although these evolutionary relics are still available, they are not widely used and cannot be used to flow text around an image.

You can assign vertical spacing to a selected image in the Property inspector by entering a value (in pixels) in the V Space field. Assign horizontal spacing by entering a value (in pixels) in the H Space field (**Figure 45d**).

Tip

A good standard setting for keeping images from bumping into text is 6 pixels of vertical spacing and 6 pixels of horizontal spacing.

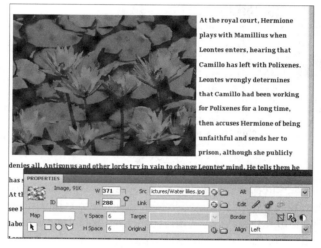

Figure 45d Assigning 6 pixels of vertical spacing and 6 pixels of horizontal spacing around an image.

Spacing around selected images appears as a blue line in the Document window. The blue line will disappear when you deselect the image.

#46 Creating Image Maps

You can launch links from either text or images. A single image, however, can contain more than one link. Breaking an image into sections, each with its own link definition, is called *creating an image map.* Image maps are used in a variety of Web graphics. One obvious example is an actual map, where a visitor can click a location (such as a state, city, or restaurant) and launch a link that opens a new page to display the area of the map where the user clicked.

Image maps are often used to create navigation bars from a single image. A wide, thin graphic that stretches across the width of a page, for instance, can be divided into many links by creating multiple image maps on the same graphic.

Image map sections can be rectangles (including squares), ovals (including circles), or polygons (multisided shapes).

To create an image map from an image already embedded in your page, follow these steps:

1. Select the image to which the image map will be applied.

2. Click the Rectangular, Oval, or Polygonal Hotspot tool in the lower-left corner of the Property inspector (**Figure 46a**).

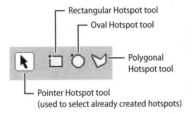

Figure 46a Hotspot tools in the Property inspector.

3. Draw a rectangle or oval by simply clicking and dragging the image with the appropriate Hotspot tool selected. Polygonal hotspots are a bit trickier. To define a polygonal hotspot, choose the Polygonal

(continued on next page)

Hotspot tool, and then click *(do not click and drag)* spots on the image. The hotspot is defined as you create additional points (**Figure 46b**).

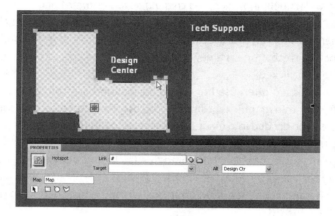

Figure 46b Defining a polygonal hotspot.

4. You can move a defined hotspot by selecting it with the Pointer Hotspot tool and dragging the whole hotspot. To delete a hotspot, select it with the Pointer Hotspot tool and press the Delete key. To resize a hotspot, select a single handle and drag it (**Figure 46c**).

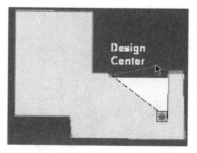

Figure 46c Editing the shape of a polygonal hotspot.

5. As soon as you finish drawing a hotspot, or if you select a hotspot with the Pointer Hotspot tool, the Property inspector adapts and displays properties just for the selected hotspot, not for the entire selected image (**Figure 46d**).

In the Map field, you can name your map (or just accept the default name). In the Link field, click the blue Browse for File (folder) icon to navigate to a file in your Web site or enter a URL in the field. In the Target field, choose _blank if you want the link to open in a new browser window. If you don't want to open the link in a new browser window, don't enter anything in the Target field. You can define a separate Alt tag for the hotspot by selecting a tag from the Alt menu. Or, you can enter alternate text in the Alt field in the Property inspector. (For an explanation of Alt tags, see #43, "Defining Alt Tags for Images").

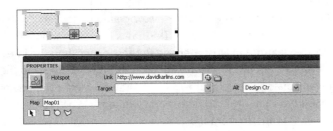

Figure 46d Defining a hotspot.

Hotspots are widely supported in browsers, but they appear differently in different browsers. Like everything involved in your Web pages, you should try to test your hotspots in several viewing environments.

Zoom to Draw Hotspots

Drawing hotspots is a technique made much easier by Dreamweaver CS4's ability to zoom in (or out). To zoom in, go to the Document window and choose View > Zoom In. To zoom to a set magnification, choose View > Magnification, and then choose a magnification percent from the submenu.

By zooming in, you can draw accurate hotspots on an image. When you're finished drawing, choose View > Magnification > 100% to view the page as it will be seen in a browser window.

#47 Placing Photoshop Files in Web Pages

Copy and Paste Images into Dreamweaver

When you copy and paste images into Dreamweaver, the Image Preview dialog launches, and you can use it to save the pasted image as a GIF, JPEG, or PNG file.

Unfortunately, the ability to copy and paste from Adobe Photoshop is not yet (in CS4) implemented for Adobe Illustrator vector images.

Saving Photoshop files to a JPEG, GIF, or PNG format is easily done within Photoshop, which shares with Adobe Illustrator the Save for Web and Devices utility—a powerful, interactive environment for fine-tuning the conversion of non-Web-compatible formats to Web-compatible formats. One obvious limitation to this system is that Web designers without access to Photoshop can't handle Photoshop files. Or, for those designers with access to Photoshop, this requires launching a separate program to convert the Photoshop file to a JPEG, GIF, or PNG format.

Dreamweaver CS4 uses the Image Preview dialog to convert Photoshop files to Web-compatible formats. Designers who are familiar with the Save to Web features in Illustrator and Photoshop will find the interface familiar, and Web designers who are used to Fireworks will find the Image Preview dialog very similar to that in Fireworks. With the Image Preview dialog, you can place a Photoshop file directly in a Web page in Dreamweaver. Or, you can copy and paste selected content directly from Photoshop to Dreamweaver.

When Dreamweaver converts a file to a JPEG, GIF, or PNG format, the original Photoshop file remains. Photoshop files that are converted to Web-compatible file formats in Dreamweaver display a small PS (Photoshop) icon in the Edit area of the Property inspector when the image is selected. Click the Photoshop icon to edit the Photoshop source file.

To place a Photoshop file in a Dreamweaver Web page, follow these steps:

1. Click in the Web page at the point at which the image will be inserted.

2. Select Insert > Image. The Select Image Source dialog appears. Navigate to a Photoshop (PSD) file, and click the Choose button. *Or*, you can copy an image from Photoshop into your operating system clipboard, and then paste that image into the Dreamweaver Document window.

3. After you place a Photoshop (PSD) file *or* copy and paste selected content from Photoshop into Dreamweaver, the Photoshop image appears in the Image Preview dialog. An easy way to compare file formats and settings is to switch to the 4-Up view, where you can see and compare different options. To view four options at once, click the 4-Up icon to display four different preview windows (**Figure 47a**).

File tab

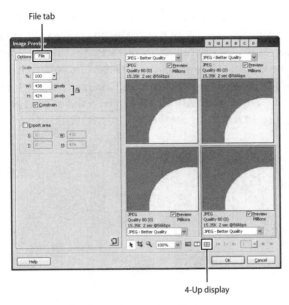

4-Up display

Figure 47a Displaying four preview windows.

4. Use the Pointer tool to select a window. When you click and drag within a window, the Pointer tool becomes a Grabber hand, and you can move around the image (**Figure 47b**).

Pointer tool / Grabber hand

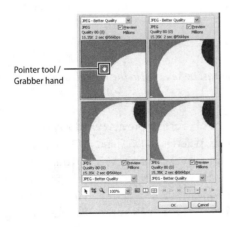

Figure 47b Exploring an image in a preview window.

(*continued on next page*)

#47: Placing Photoshop Files in Web Pages

5. The Set Magnification pop-up menu in the Image Preview dialog allows you to zoom in and out (use the Alt key in Windows or the Option key on Macs to zoom out). Or, you can zoom interactively using the Zoom In/Out tool. The Crop tool is used to crop an image in a selected preview window. To crop an image, click the Crop tool, and then click and drag on any of the corner or side anchors to crop the image before conversion (**Figure 47c**).

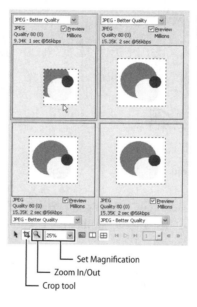

Set Magnification
Zoom In/Out
Crop tool

Figure 47c Cropping a Photoshop image before converting it to a Web-compatible format.

Note

The Export area check box must be selected in the File tab before you can convert.

6. In the Options tab, select one of your four preview windows and experiment with different formats, palettes (for GIF and PNG formats), and settings. As you adjust image quality, color palettes, and other options, you'll see a preview of the generated image in the selected preview window. Each preview window has a pop-up menu from which you can select from seven presets. These presets provide a good range of options and are a good way to experiment with image conversion if you are not fluent in image file format features. Each window also displays the file size and estimated download time for the conversion (**Figure 47d**).

Selected preview estimated download time ⎯

Selected preview file size ⎯

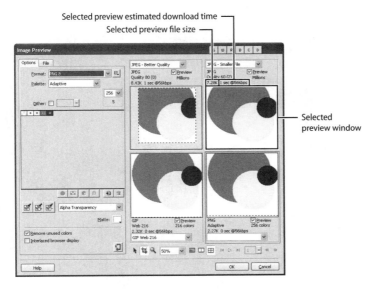

Selected preview window

Figure 47d Previewing four different image conversion options for high-quality JPEG, smaller-file JPEG, 8-color PNG, and GIF.

7. After you define the image format and settings for the converted image, click OK. The Save Web Image dialog opens. Assign a filename in the Save As box, and click Save. If the Image Tag Accessibility Attributes dialog opens, enter a short description of the image in the Alternate text box and click OK.

CHAPTER EIGHT

Creating and Using Custom Templates and Libraries

If your Web site is just a handful of pages, you can manage the content on each page more or less independently. That is, you can open each page, one at a time, and edit content.

However, when your site is more complex than just a few pages (and most are), you'll find Dreamweaver's features for managing embedded site content essential.

Dreamweaver allows you to create page elements, such as navigation bars, page banners, icons, and bits of text (for example, a copyright notice), and then embed these elements in any of your site's pages. These elements can be text, images, or a combination of text and images. There are two different kinds of site elements in Dreamweaver:

- Template pages provide a common design for all pages to which they are attached.

- Library items are objects that are embedded in any number of pages.

Both template pages and library items are *updatable sitewide*. This means that if you embed a logo, copyright notice, text, or image (or a combination of text and images) in your pages and you edit the template or library item that defines that object, *all pages* that are created from the template or that have the library item embedded in them will update automatically.

This chapter explains how to create template pages, how to generate new pages from a template, how to define library items, and how to embed library items in pages.

#48 Creating Template Pages

The central concept in creating and using template pages is that they include *editable* and *noneditable* regions. Noneditable template page regions are parts of the page that are defined in the template; they can only be edited in the template file. Once they are edited, they apply to all pages with which the template is associated.

Let's explore a typical template page. The page might have a banner across the top, a navigation bar on the left, and a copyright/navigation bar at the bottom. The template defines these elements. A region in the middle of the page could function as an editable region and would have different content on every page on the site (**Figure 48a**).

Figure 48a   A page template with space for editable content.

To create a template page, choose File > New to open the New Document dialog. Select Blank Page in the category (left side) column of the dialog, and click the HTML Template in the Page Type page column. If you want, you can use one of the available layouts in the Layout column as a basis for your template, but normally you'll want to select <none> in the Layout column to design your template from scratch. Click the Create button (**Figure 48b**). The template page opens.

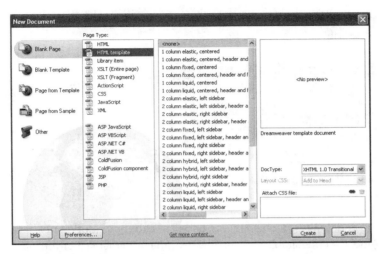

Figure 48b Creating a new template.

The Document window for a template page looks just like the Document window for a regular page except that <<Template>> appears in the title bar of the window.

Tip
Just to review where you are in the process: At this stage, you are defining the template page. This page will then be used to generate an unlimited number of actual site pages based on the template you are defining.

There are two steps to creating a template page. First, create all the *noneditable* elements that will appear on *every* page. Second, create the editable regions.

When you define template pages, you don't draw editable regions. You take existing page elements (such as a table, table cell, or CSS layer), and you make these elements editable when you use the template to generate new pages. Therefore, the standard strategy for creating a template page is to first create a page layout using either CSS layers or tables. You can then place noneditable content in tables or table cells (if you are designing with tables) or in a CSS layer.

To make an element on the page—like a table, table cell, or AP object—into an editable region, click inside the element, and then choose Insert > Template Objects > Editable Region. The New Editable Region dialog opens.

Optional Editable Regions

You can include optional editable regions in a template. These regions might or might not be on a page, depending on the discretion of the designer of the individual page. For example, you might make it possible for content authors to include an image on a page, but you might not want to display an empty image box if no image is available. In this case, you could include an optional editable region where the image would appear—if there was one.

Enter a name for the region in the Name field, and then click the OK button to define the region (**Figure 48c**).

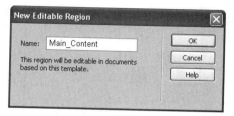

Figure 48c Naming an editable region on a template page.

In addition to editable regions, template pages can (but do not have to) include noneditable content. Any text, image, or media that you place on a template page that is *not in an editable region* becomes part of every page generated by that template.

You might, for example, have copyright information that appears at the bottom of every page generated by the template, or you might have contact information or a navigation bar on every page. You can include on a template page anything you can put on a regular Web page. Just keep in mind that any content that is not in an editable region will appear on *every* page generated using the template you are defining.

Once you have defined a template page with a noneditable region (if you want to make it part of the template) and at least one editable region, you're ready to save the page and use it to generate an unlimited number of pages. Save the page by choosing File > Save. The Save As Template dialog opens. Enter a short description in the Description field and enter a filename in the Save as field (**Figure 48d**).

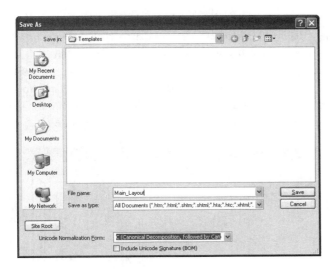

Figure 48d Saving a template.

Note

By default, Dreamweaver automatically creates a Templates folder on your site and will save all template pages in that folder. Dreamweaver templates are saved with a .dwt file extension.

Repeating Regions

Repeating regions are used for highly complex commercial data-driven sites. They allow data to pour into a template page and for editable regions like tables to expand to accommodate the data. Again, this kind of site development is complex and beyond the scope of this book. However, if you were embedding a table to display the results of a search query that might have any number of results (between 1 and 10, for instance), you could design a repeating region that would display anywhere from 1 to 10 search results. You can even embed editable regions inside other editable regions.

#49 Generating New Pages from Custom Templates

To create a new page from a template, choose File > New to open the New Document dialog. In the New Document dialog, click the Page from Template category on the left side of the dialog. In the Site column, click the site on which you are working (if you have more than one). In the Templates for Site column, click (don't double-click) one of the templates. You can preview any available template page by clicking it to see a thumbnail image of the template in the preview area of the dialog (**Figure 49a**).

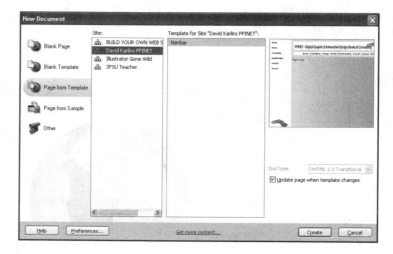

Figure 49a Viewing templates for a Web site.

Tip
The Update page when template changes check box is selected by default. Most of the point of designing with templates is that when you edit the template, all pages generated by that template will update to reflect the changes to the template file. So, normally you will leave this check box selected.

After you select a template, click the Create button in the dialog to generate a new page. The new page will include all noneditable content (images, text, or media) that is part of the template. To enter unique content for the generated page, click in the editable region for the template and enter text, images, or other content. If there are multiple editable regions, click in every region and enter content (**Figure 49b**).

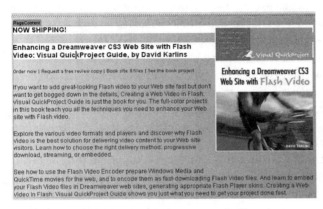

Figure 49b Entering an image and text in an editable region.

Note

By default, editable regions are named sequentially—EditRegion1, EditRegion2, and so on—as they are generated. But you can rename them with custom names that are more descriptive by clicking on the editable region title (like EditRegion1) and entering a new name (like Page Content or Photo Goes Here).

After editing the editable region on a template page, save the page by choosing File > Save. Assign a filename and save the page as you would any Web page.

#50 Updating Templates

Your Web site consists of 2,304,451 pages. Okay, let's say it consists of 230 pages. In any case, consider this scenario: You need to change an element that appears on every page. It might be a newly designed company logo, an updated news notice, or a drastic personnel change.

In any case, you can easily update all the affected pages on your site in minutes by editing the template on which your site pages are based.

Then comes the slow part: After you update a template, you still need to upload all changed pages to your server. Because this is confusing to many people, I've included a separate how-to at the end of this chapter on managing template updates at a remote server (see #53, "Uploading Templates and Library Items").

You can easily open and edit a template either from the File menu or from an open page that is associated with the template. If you have a page open that was generated from the template you want to edit, choose Modify > Templates > Open Attached Template (**Figure 50a**).

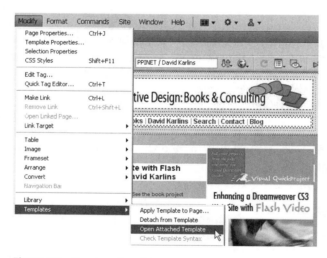

Figure 50a Opening a template page.

If a page associated with your template is not open, choose File > Open and navigate to the template file in the Open dialog.

With the template page open, edit the noneditable regions (that is, any region that is not defined as an editable region). After you edit the page content, choose File > Save. The Update Template Files dialog opens. The

Creating and Using Custom Templates and Libraries

dialog lists all files generated from the template you are saving. If you only want to update some of the pages generated from the template, select the files to update. Then click the Update button to apply the changes in the template to all (or selected) pages (**Figure 50b**).

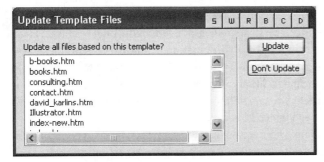

Figure 50b Saving a template page and updating files.

The Update Pages dialog then appears. Here, you can select the Show log check box to generate a list of affected pages (**Figure 50c**). When the update process is completed, click the Close button to close the Update Pages dialog.

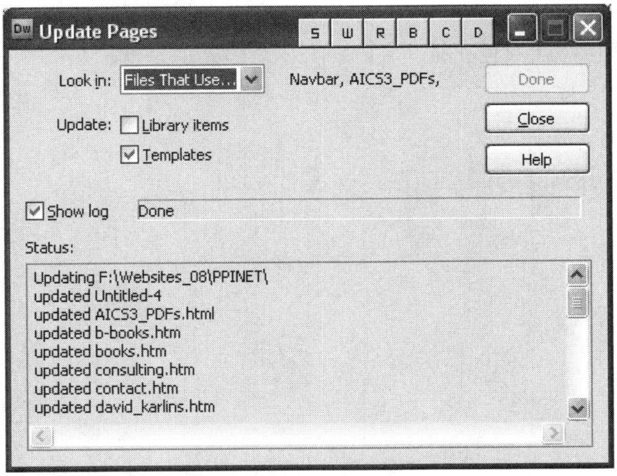

Figure 50c Viewing a log of updated pages.

#51 Creating and Placing Library Items

Library Items or Templates?

Library items and templates often provide alternative ways of accomplishing similar tasks. Both can be updated. For example, you could create all pages on a Web site using a template that has company contact information on the page as noneditable content. If the company moves, you can update the address on every page generated from a template by making a change to the noneditable content in the template.

Another approach would be to embed company contact information as a library item. When the contact information changes, you can update the library item and the change will be reflected in the content of every page in which the item is embedded.

Library items are like templates in that they are associated with pages, and they update sitewide. They are different in that library items are *embedded in a page*, and they can be placed in pages generated by templates, in template pages, or in just a regular Web page. Another way to think of it is that templates are entire pages, whereas library items are just individual elements that can be inserted into any page.

Library items can be text, images, or even media plug-ins (like a Flash animation), or they can be a combination of these. For example, if you want to place an article on every page or on several pages, you could embed the article as a library item. When the time comes to update or change the article, you can edit the library item and update the article on every Web page in which it is embedded.

You can define a library item in two ways. You can drag content from an existing page into the Library window, or you can define library content from scratch in the Library window.

To drag existing content into the Library window, follow these steps:

1. Choose Window > Assets to view the Assets panel.

2. In the column on the left side of the Assets panel, click the Library icon (the last icon in the column). Any existing library items will display (**Figure 51a**).

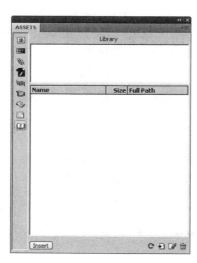

Figure 51a Viewing the Library category of the Assets panel.

3. Click and drag to select the content on your page that will become a library item. Drag the content to the top or bottom window in the Library category of the Assets panel (**Figure 51b**).

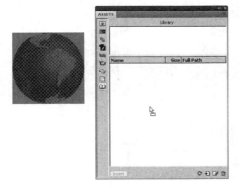

Figure 51b Dragging content to the Library category of the Assets panel.

Note

When you drag content to the Library category, a warning dialog alerts you that the content may not appear the same when it is embedded in a page. See the sidebar "Library Items Adopt CSS Styles" for an explanation of this occurrence.

4. Enter a name for the new library item by clicking the item in the Names list at the bottom of the Library category of the Assets panel and entering a new name.

You can also create a library item from scratch. There are four icons at the bottom of the Library category of the Assets panel (**Figure 51c**):

- The Refresh Site List icon generates an updated list of library items associated with the open Web site.

- The New Library Item icon creates a new library item.

- The Edit icon opens a window to edit the selected library item.

- The Delete icon deletes the selected library item.

Library Items Adopt CSS Styles

Library items may look different on different pages because they adopt the CSS styles of the page in which they are embedded. Normally, this is no big deal. If all the pages on your Web site use the same CSS styles for formatting, the embedded library item will look the same on every page.

But there's another wrinkle in the process: If you edit a CSS style, it will change how the embedded library items with that style attached to them will appear on Web pages. This is not a bad thing; it just means that library items are governed by an external style sheet applied to a page the same way other page objects are.

See Chapter 9, "Working with External Style Sheets," for an explanation of how to manage sitewide formatting with CSS.

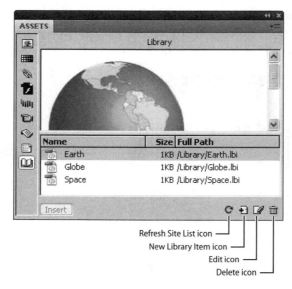

Figure 51c Icons in the Library category of the Assets panel.

To create a new library item, follow these steps:

1. To generate a new library item, first create any kind of content (including text or images) in the Document window. Select that content and drag it into the top half of the Library category of the Assets panel. As you do, a new library item named Untitled appears in the bottom half of the Library category of the Assets panel.

2. Create a new name for the library item by clicking Untitled in the bottom half of the Library category of the Assets panel and entering a new name for the new library item.

3. To create additional library items, click the New Library Item icon at the bottom of the Library category in the Assets panel.

After you create a library item, you can drag it from the Library category of the Assets panel to any page on your Web site. Do this by simply dragging the library item to an open page in the Document window (**Figure 51d**).

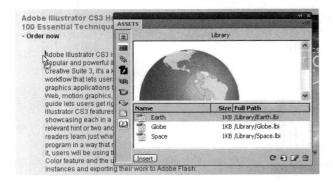

Figure 51d Dragging a library item to a page.

Library Items Can Include Anything

Library items are really HTML snippets (blocks of HTML code) that are embedded in other HTML pages.

Library items are saved with an .lbi file extension. They are proprietary objects in Dreamweaver—you can't edit a library item if you open a site with Adobe GoLive or another Web editing tool.

#52 Updating Library Items

When you edit a library item, the item will update on every page in which it is embedded. To edit a library item, click the item in the Library category of the Assets panel, and then click the Edit icon at the bottom of the panel. The library item opens as a new document, which looks like and can be edited just as if it were a Dreamweaver Web page. The difference is that Library items are saved with an .lbi extension (**Figure 52a**).

Figure 52a A library item open and being edited in a Library window.

The Library Item window is just like the Document window except that it is used to edit library items. You can edit in the Library Item window just as you would in the Document window. After you edit the library item in the Library Item window, choose File > Save to save your changes. The Update Library Items dialog appears with a list of all pages in which the library item is embedded.

You can select some of the pages in the list to update or simply click the Update button to update the entire list (**Figure 52b**).

Figure 52b Updating pages with a library item embedded in them.

After Dreamweaver finishes updating pages with embedded library items, the Update Pages dialog appears. You can select the Show log check box to see a list of all updated pages (**Figure 52c**).

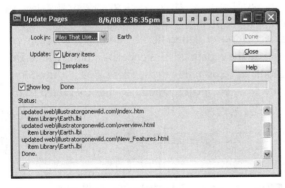

Figure 52c Viewing a list of updated pages with an embedded library item.

#53 Uploading Templates and Library Items

Dreamweaver Manages Files, Folders, and Links

When Dreamweaver inserts a library item on a page in *any* subfolder (directory) on a site, it updates any links in that library item relative to the location where the file is saved. And, when a page made from a template is saved in any subfolder, the links are updated relative to the saved location.

You'll notice that the Template folder and the Library Item folder don't even get uploaded to the server. They are used to *generate* pages only. Library items and templates are not actually Web pages and don't get uploaded to your server. Management of links sitewide is one of the biggest reasons to use Dreamweaver and one of the tasks it's really good at doing.

One of the things my clients and students (and fellow developers) find most confusing in Dreamweaver is managing changes to templates and library items on a remote server. Here's why: When you edit a library item (or template), all pages associated with that library item or template are automatically updated *on your local site*. These pages are *not* automatically updated *at the remote server*. Because this can be confusing and frustrating, I'll walk you through the process.

When you save changes to an edited template, you are prompted to update all pages generated by the template. When you edit and save changes to a library item, the Update Library Items dialog appears, prompting you to update all changes in pages in which the library item is embedded. Clicking the Update button in the Update Library Items dialog updates all pages in which the library item appears.

You *cannot* update the pages on your remote server by simply uploading the revised template or library page. You update the pages on your local server first, and then you *upload all changed pages* to the remote server.

How do you keep track of which pages need to be uploaded to the remote server after you edit them by changing a template or library item? One way is to actually pay attention to the logs generated by Dreamweaver that list the changed pages. These logs can be copied and pasted into a word processor for easier management.

I usually use this trick: After updating files by editing a template or library item, sort the files in the expanded Files panel by modified date. Do this by clicking the Modified column title in the Files panel (**Figure 53a**). You can then Shift-click to select recently modified files that need to be uploaded.

Local Files	Size	Type	Modified
⊟ 📁 Site - Illustrator Gone Wild (C:\Websites\Illustrator...		Folder	8/6/2008 2:19 PM
⊞ 📁 Library		Folder	8/6/2008 2:34 PM
⊟ 📁 web		Folder	8/6/2008 1:51 PM
⊟ 📁 illustratorgonewild.com		Folder	8/6/2008 2:34 PM
📄 New_Features.html	1KB	Firefox Docu...	8/6/2008 2:34 PM
📄 index.htm	14KB	Firefox Docu...	8/6/2008 2:34 PM
📄 overview.html	1KB	Firefox Docu...	8/6/2008 2:34 PM
📄 Bang-sample.ai	2.78MB	AI File	6/22/2008 8:59 PM
📄 Seasons Greetings Thumb.JPG	8KB	JPEG Image	7/4/2007 12:00 AM
📄 bg_grad-1.jpg	1KB	JPEG Image	7/4/2007 12:00 AM

Figure 53a Files sorted by the date they were modified; new files to be uploaded are selected.

With the files to be uploaded selected, click the Put File(s) icon in the Files panel to upload the files to the remote server (**Figure 53b**).

Put Files

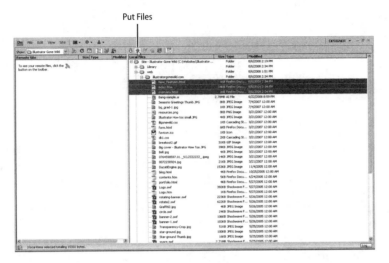

Figure 53b Uploading selected (recently changed) files.

Managing Local-to-Remote Transfers

Dreamweaver provides some sophisticated tools for uploading files to the remote server that match various criteria, including uploading all files that are newer on the local site than they are on the remote server.

These tools are explored in Chapter 1. See "Defining a Remote Site," #5, and "Uploading To a Remote Site," #6.

CHAPTER NINE

Working with External Style Sheets

External style sheets are separate files with .css filename extensions that are linked to HTML Web pages. Those CSS files define page attributes for every page to which they are linked.

External style sheets have many powerful advantages that make them ubiquitous in professional Web sites:

- They can be applied to any number of pages.

- They can be used to instantly update the look and format of every page to which they are attached.

- They ensure a uniform, global look and feel to a Web site by applying uniform formatting to every page in the site.

A single style sheet file (or sometimes a few files) stores all the information needed to format every Web page to which that style sheet is attached. When a visitor opens the HTML page to which a CSS file is attached, the browser automatically looks to the CSS file to find out how to display the page. This process does not take any noticeable time. Visitors to your Web site simply see a page with formatting, even though the formatting rules are stored in a separate (CSS) file.

Within a Web site, you can use CSS to apply uniform formatting to:

- Body tags that define pagewide formatting, such as page background, margins, and default font color, type, and size

- HTML tags ranging from images to tables

- Links with special attributes

- Special printable page formatting

#54 Creating an External Style Sheet

The easiest way to generate a CSS (style sheet) file in Dreamweaver is to create a new style. As you do, you'll have the option of including that style in a new CSS file. In the following steps, you'll define a style and save it in a new style sheet. These steps can be adapted to generate a CSS file using any tag as the initiating style.

1. In the Document window, click the New CSS Rule icon at the bottom of the CSS Styles panel (**Figure 54a**). The New CSS Rule dialog appears.

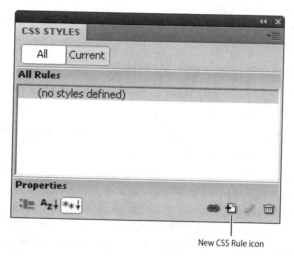

New CSS Rule icon

Figure 54a The New CSS Rule icon in the CSS Styles panel.

2. In the Selector Type area of the dialog, choose the type of style you want to define.

   • Choose Class to apply formatting rules, which are independent of tags, to any selected text. If you are creating a Class style, enter a name for your style in the Name box.

   • Choose ID to define a style that will apply to just one HTML tag.

   • Choose Tag to define formatting for HTML elements, such as headings, paragraphs, images, tables, or pages. When the Tag radio button is selected, every HTML tag appears in a pull-down menu next to the Tag field.

Note
Heading tags that are listed in the Property inspector as Heading 1, Head-ing 2, and so on are listed by their HTML tag names here (e.g., h1 equals the Heading 1 tag).

- Choose Compound to let Dreamweaver select a style type auto-matically based on the HTML tag you have selected.

3. Choose (New Style Sheet File) from the Rule Definition pop-up menu (**Figure 54b**).

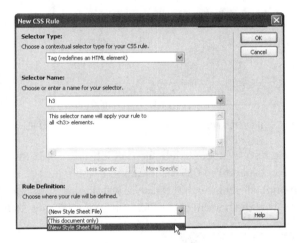

Figure 54b Generating a new style sheet.

4. Click OK in the New CSS Rule dialog. The Save Style Sheet File As dialog appears. This is a typical Save As dialog except that it automatically generates a CSS file with a .css file extension and translates any format-ting you define into CSS coding. Navigate to the folder in which you want to save the style sheet and enter a filename in the Save As field. Then click Save to generate the new CSS file.

5. After you click Save, the CSS Rule Definition dialog for the style you are defining opens. Different categories in the Category list offer format-ting options for different kinds of page elements. Now, simply note that there is a wide array of formatting options available and that whatever formatting options you define will be encoded into the CSS file you named and saved in step 4 (**Figure 54c**).

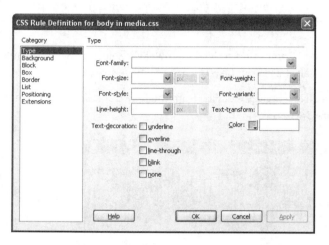

Figure 54c The CSS Rule Definition dialog.

6. After you create a style sheet file, the file is visible in the CSS Styles panel. When you expand the CSS file (click the triangle next to it to toggle to expand), all styles within the style will display. Formatting attributes display at the bottom of the CSS Styles panel (**Figure 54d**).

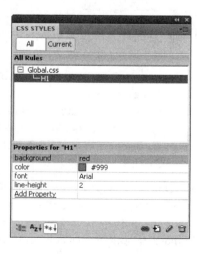

Figure 54d Viewing a CSS style in an attached style sheet in the CSS Styles panel.

After creating a CSS file, you add styles to the file *without* creating a new style sheet. So, once you have created your first style and generated a CSS file, the *next* time you create a new style, click the New CSS Rule icon in the CSS Styles panel, but this time simply accept your existing CSS file in the New CSS Rule dialog (**Figure 54e**).

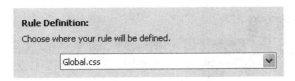

Figure 54e Defining additional styles for an existing CSS file in the New CSS Rule dialog.

Should You Apply CSS to Table and Image Tags?

Maybe. Keep in mind that if you apply a style to the Table tag—for example, a yellow background color—that style applies to *all* tables on your site (assuming you are using an external style sheet). I find this a bit heavy handed. I like to apply different background colors to tables within my site, so I usually don't define a table style. When I manage very large sites, I usually define a CSS style for the Table tag because I don't want or need to custom define background colors for every table.

On the other hand, I normally define a style for images. I'll use a style to define the border thickness and color that appears around the images. I like to keep this style standard throughout my site.

#55 Attaching an External Style Sheet

As soon as you define a style in an external style sheet, that style is available to be attached to any new or existing page. To attach a style sheet to a page, open the page, and then click the Attach Style Sheet (link) icon in the CSS Styles panel (**Figure 55a**). The Attach External Style Sheet dialog opens.

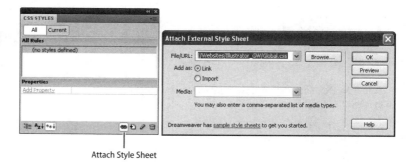

Attach Style Sheet

Figure 55a Attaching a style sheet to an open page.

Navigate to your CSS file in the File/URL field, choose the Add as Link option, and click OK to attach the style sheet.

Once you have attached a style sheet to multiple pages on your Web site (even thousands of pages), you can instantly update the appearance of the pages by editing your style sheet. Simply follow these steps:

1. Open any page that has the style sheet attached.

2. In the CSS Styles panel, select the All tab. If necessary, click the Expand/Collapse icon next to the CSS file to display a list of styles. Select any style to edit that style.

3. You can edit the CSS file in two ways:

   • Double-click on the style in the top half of the CSS Styles panel to open the CSS Rule Definition dialog. When you click OK in the CSS Rule Definition dialog, the changes are automatically applied to all pages to which the edited style sheet file is attached.

   • Click any style attribute in the bottom half of the CSS Styles panel and edit the style right in the panel. After you edit the style, note that the linked CSS file displays as a tab in the Document window with an asterisk (*) next to it. You need to select that tab and save the CSS file (choose File > Save) to save the edited CSS file and apply the new formatting to all files to which the CSS file is attached (**Figure 55b**).

Figure 55b A CSS file displayed as a tab ready to be saved.

#56 Formatting Links with CSS

By default, links are displayed in blue type (or blue borders for images). Visited links are purple, and active links (ones in the process of being opened) are red. And, by default, all links display with underlining. You can customize the appearance and behavior of links using CSS. CSS formatting is applied to links so ubiquitously that sophisticated Web browsers expect to find features like rollover display or nonunderlined links on sites.

CSS formatting allows you to define four link states. In addition to the three HTML states (regular, visited, and active links), CSS can define a fourth state—hover. Hover state displays when a visitor hovers the mouse cursor over the link.

Many style approaches are used for hover link formatting. Sometimes, designers turn off underlining for all other link states but will have it appear when a visitor hovers over a link (**Figure 56a**). Other times, designers define a color or background-display change when a link is hovered over.

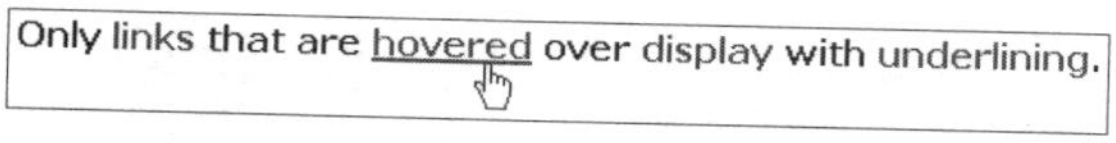

Only links that are <u>hovered</u> over display with underlining.

Figure 56a An underscore appears under the hovered-over link but is not visible in links that are not hovered over.

Normally, you will *not* define font or font size to link style definitions. That's because links inherit the font and font size of the HTML formatting tag assigned to the text. For example, Heading 1 (h1) text might include text that is a link. Or, paragraph text might include some text that functions as a link. In either case, the font and font size will not change for the link text.

What often *will* change is font color and maybe font attributes like underlining or background. So, when you define CSS styles for links, you will normally avoid defining font or font size and instead define font color and special attributes (like underlining or background).

To create a CSS formatting *rule* (style) for links on a page (or in a Web site via an external CSS file), follow these steps:

1. With a page open, click the New CSS Rule icon in the CSS Styles panel. The New CSS Rule dialog opens.

2. From the Selector Type pop-up menu, choose Compound. From the Selector Name pop-up menu, choose one of the four link states: link, visited, hover, or active (**Figure 56b**).

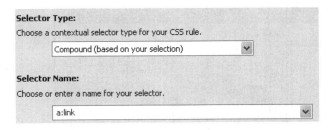

Figure 56b Defining an unvisited link style in the New CSS Rule dialog.

Note
You will define each of the four link states separately. Link (unvisited link), visited, hover, and active are each a unique style. For these link styles to be interpreted correctly in browsers, you need to create them in the order listed above. If you need to reorder styles, you can click on any style in the CSS Styles panel and drag it up or down in the panel to reorder.

3. In the Rule Definition area of the dialog, choose a style sheet file from the menu.

4. Click OK in the New CSS Rule dialog to open the CSS Rule Definition dialog for the link state you are defining. The formatting options you are likely to use for a link state are as follows:

- **Type category:** Allows you to define a color for the selected link state using the Color box. The check boxes in the Decoration area allow you to turn underlining on or off. By default, links are

(continued on next page)

underlined, so select the None check box to turn *off* underlining. Simply deselecting the Underline check box will not turn off underlining (**Figure 56c**).

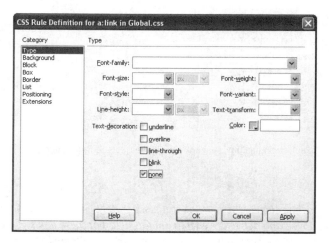

Figure 56c Turning off underlining for a link state.

- **Background category:** Allows you to define a background color or image behind the selected text.

5. After you define a CSS link style, click OK to automatically apply it to an external style sheet or to your page (depending on the selection you made in the Define in section of the New CSS Rule dialog when you began defining the style). However, you will not see the effect of any link state other than link (unvisited) until you preview your page in a browser. To do this, choose File > Preview in Browser, and if more than one browser is available, choose a browser from the submenu.

#57 Defining Page Properties with CSS

The Body tag is a special tag. It underlies all other tags on a page. Think of the Body tag as the tag you will use to define page layout options such as page margins and background color (or pattern file). The Body tag also defines default font characteristics and other attributes that apply to an entire page.

A CSS style applied to the Body tag is a powerful, sitewide formatting tool. You can actually define most of the formatting for your site using the Body tag. Also, since the Body tag defines page background color, this is another way in which this one style can control much of your site's appearance.

To define a style for the Body tag that establishes a default font, a page background color, and margin specs, follow these steps:

1. Click the New CSS Rule icon in the CSS Styles panel. The New CSS Rule dialog opens.

2. In the Selector Type area of the dialog, choose Tag. From the Selector Name pop-up menu, choose body (**Figure 57a**).

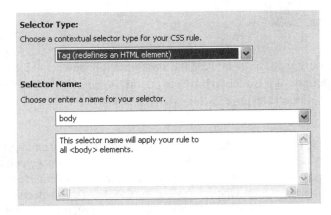

Figure 57a Defining a Body tag in the New CSS Rule dialog.

3. In the Rule Definition area of the dialog, choose the CSS file you are editing from the pop-up menu.

4. Click OK in the New CSS Rule dialog to open the CSS Rule Definition dialog for your Body tag. In the Type category, choose a font from the Font pop-up menu.

(continued on next page)

Don't Define Too Much

Normally, when you define a Body tag, you won't define font size or attributes such as italics or boldface. Remember, a Body tag provides the *basic* default formatting for text. You'll want different tag styles to look differently, and normally you'll define font size as you define the Paragraph tag (p) and heading tags (h1, h2, and so on). Any attributes you define for these tags will override the Body tag definition.

For example, if you defined the Body tag to display default text in dark-gray Arial font, then *all* styles included in the style sheet would by default appear in dark-gray Arial font. Heading 1 (h1) text would be larger than Paragraph (p) text. All text would be dark-gray Arial font by default.

5. In the Background category of the CSS Rule Definition dialog, choose a swatch from the Background color area to select a background color for your page(s) if you want something other than the default white color (**Figure 57b**).

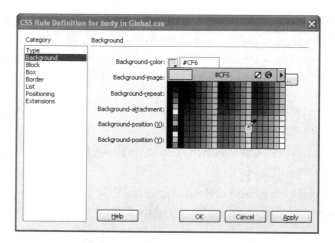

Figure 57b Defining page background color.

6. If you want, you can define a tiling background image instead of a background color. Do this in the Background category by clicking the Browse button to locate and choose an image file.

Tip

By default, background images tile horizontally (on the Y-axis) and vertically (on the X-axis). In other words, they fill the entire page background when you attach them to a Body tag style. You can use the Repeat pop-up menu in the Background category of the CSS Rule Definition dialog to change the default settings. Options include Repeat-Y, which repeats the image only along the Y-axis (vertically), or Repeat-X, which repeats the image horizontally. Or, you can choose No-Repeat to not repeat the background image at all.

7. Different browsers display different default page margins. To define a set margin, select the Box category in the CSS Rule Definition dialog and enter values for top, left, bottom, and right margins (**Figure 57c**).

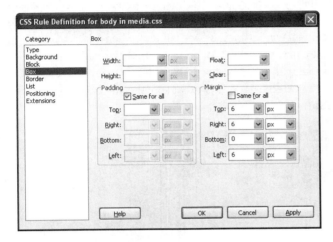

Figure 57c Defining page margins.

8. After you finish defining attributes for the Body tag, click OK in the CSS Rule Definition dialog to save the changes to your Body tag as part of the linked CSS file.

#58 Defining CSS for Printable Pages

Many times you will want to define different styles for printed pages than you use for monitor display. For example, you might change a light-colored font to black for printing or remove page or table background images.

You do this by creating and attaching a separate CSS file—a separate external style sheet—that holds print formatting rules. You can also preview in the Document window how a page will look when printed.

To define a new style sheet for printer output, you can create an external style sheet with CSS tag styles, link styles, or even class styles. Then you name the external style sheet that contains the print styles print.css (**Figure 58a**).

Figure 58a Creating a new CSS file called print.css.

Tip

Review the other techniques in this chapter for all the information you need to create an external style sheet.

After you define a distinct set of printable styles in the print.css style sheet file, attach the print.css file as the printer style sheet:

1. Open the Web page to which the printer CSS styles will be attached.

2. In the CSS Styles panel, click the Attach Style Sheet (link) icon.

3. In the File/URL field of the Attach External Style Sheet dialog, click Browse and navigate to the print.css file. Click OK (Windows) or Choose (Mac). The Attach External Style Sheet dialog appears. In the Add as area, leave the Link radio button selected.

4. From the Media pop-up menu, choose print (**Figure 58b**).

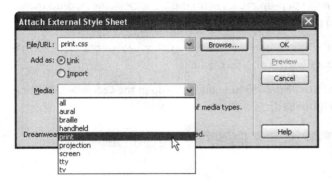

Figure 58b Defining print.css as the printer style sheet.

To preview your printer styles, click the Render Print Media Type icon in the Style Rendering toolbar (**Figure 58c**). If the Style Rendering toolbar is not visible, choose View > Toolbars > Style Rendering.

Style Rendering toolbar

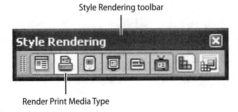

Render Print Media Type

Figure 58c Style Rendering toolbar.

One class style attribute that is only relevant to print style sheets is the page break attribute. To define a page break in the printed version of a Web page, follow these steps:

1. Open the Web page to which the printer CSS styles will be attached.

2. Click to place your insertion point where the page break should occur on the printed version of the Web page.

3. Click the New CSS Rule icon in the CSS Styles panel. The New CSS Rule dialog opens.

(continued on next page)

More than One CSS File Per Page?

Yes. You can attach multiple style sheets to a page and define different CSS files to different media using the same process.

4. In the Selector Type area of the dialog, choose Class (can apply to any tag) from the pop-up menu. From the Selector Name pop-up menu, choose a style name, such as page_break.

5. In the Rule Definition area of the dialog, choose your print.css external style sheet from the pop-up menu.

6. Click OK in the New CSS Rule dialog to open the CSS Rule Definition dialog (**Figure 58d**).

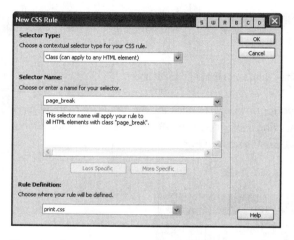

Figure 58d Creating a page break style.

7. In the CSS Rule Definition dialog, choose the Extensions category. In the After field, choose Always from the pop-up menu (**Figure 58e**).

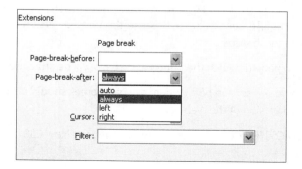

Figure 58e Defining a page break style.

After you define a page break style, you can apply it anywhere by inserting the style from the Property inspector (**Figure 58f**).

Figure 58f Inserting a page break style.

Useful Print Formatting

Useful special formatting features for printed versions of pages include the following:

- **No colored print:** Many people print documents on laser printers that print only in black.

- **No backgrounds:** They interfere with readability.

- **Different margins:** They accommodate standard 8½-inch-wide paper.

- **Page breaks:** They break content into discrete sections.

#59 Viewing Related Files

As discussed in the introduction to this chapter, external CSS style sheets are *separate files*. They are distinct from any HTML Web page to which they are attached. At the same time, they have a big impact on how pages to which they are linked appear.

To make it easy to identify linked CSS files, Dreamweaver CS4 displays these files in what can best be described as a set of subtabs in the Document window (**Figure 59**).

Figure 59 Viewing related files for an HTML page—in this case two CSS files.

To view related files, choose Related Files from the View menu.

Unsaved related files appear with an asterisk (*) after them. This is important to be aware of because sometimes when you edit CSS file attributes using the CSS Styles panel, the changes are added to the appropriate CSS file, but that file is not automatically saved (unless you close and save the HTML file to which the style sheet is attached—in which case you are prompted to save the CSS file as well). Therefore, before closing an editing session, you should select the related CSS file(s) and save it (choose File > Save).

#60 Working in Split View

In addition to identifying associated CSS files in the Related Files tab bar, Dreamweaver CS4 allows you to work in Split view. Split view is useful for editing code in one pane while viewing the results in another pane. HTML coders can type HTML code in one pane and view the results in another pane. Or, you can edit a CSS style sheet by hand in one pane and note the changes to an associated Web page in another pane.

New to CS4 is the ability to split views vertically, which is particularly handy and intuitive for looking at code and a page at the same time.

To split the Document window between Code view and Design view, choose View > Code and Design. The screen splits with one half displaying code and the other the page design (**Figure 60a**).

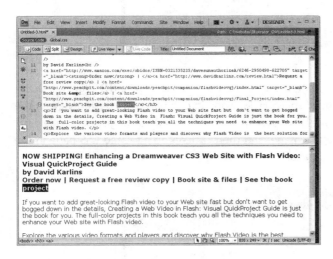

Figure 60a Viewing Code and Design.

To split the screen vertically, choose View > Split Vertically (**Figure 60b**).

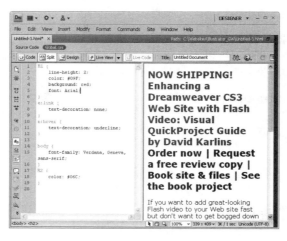

Figure 60b A vertically split screen.

By default, when you choose View > Split Code and Design, the Document window displays HTML code in one pane and Design view in the other. You can also choose to display a related CSS page in the code pane by selecting that pane, and then clicking on a related CSS page in the Related Files tab bar (**Figure 60c**).

Figure 60c Viewing a CSS for a Web page in a separate pane.

When you edit either HTML code or a related CSS page, the changes are applied to the page in Design view when you click across the pane into Design view.

CHAPTER TEN

Collecting Data in Forms

Forms provide a uniquely interactive element in a Web site. Through a form you not only *convey* content, you also *collect* content. This content can range from orders for products, feedback on site content, service requests, and subscription list sign-ups to surveys, forum discussions, and opinion polls.

Some form content is managed using scripts that run in the visitor's browser. Such scripts are referred to as *client-side* data handling. A jump menu, for example, collects data (the page a visitor to your Web site wants to go to, for example) and acts on that input (by opening a new Web page). And the client-side script does that *without* sending any data to a server. Other forms collect data and send it to a server, where scripts on the server manage the data. These are called *server-side* forms. Most form data is managed by server-side scripts. One example of a server-side script is a mailing list form. Visitors enter information (at least an email address and maybe more) into a form. That data is then stored in a database on a remote server. It can be accessed to send out mailings.

In short, this chapter explains how to design two kinds of forms:

- Forms that manage data in the browser (client-side)

- Forms that connect to scripts at a server (server-side)

In this chapter, you'll learn how to connect a form to an existing server script (but not how to program the scripts). I've also thrown in some tips on where you can find already-packaged server scripts to handle things like search forms, sign-up mailing lists, and discussion forums.

#61 Creating Jump Menus

One great example of a client-side form is a jump menu from which a visitor selects a page in your Web site from a pop-up menu. A jump menu works because script (in this case, JavaScript) acts on a form and effects an action (in this case, opening a new Web page) based on data the visitor entered into the form (the page he or she chose from the jump menu). Dreamweaver creates jump menu forms and automatically generates the required JavaScript.

Jump menus are an efficient and attractive way to allow visitors to navigate your site. You can provide a long list of target links in a jump menu without using much valuable space on your Web page (**Figure 61a**).

Figure 61a Providing a list of navigation options in a jump menu.

Jump menus use JavaScript to handle form input. In other words, when a visitor chooses a Web page (or other link, like an image file) from the jump menu, a script generated by Dreamweaver opens the selected page in a browser window. You don't need to worry about this JavaScript. But you can look at it in Code view in the Document window if you're interested in seeing what the JavaScript looks like (or, if you know how to, you can edit the generated JavaScript in Code view of the Document window).

To create a jump menu, follow these steps:

1. With a page open in the Document window, choose Insert > Form > Jump Menu. The Insert Jump Menu dialog opens.

2. In the Text field of the Insert Jump Menu dialog, enter the text that will appear in the jump menu.

Note

The text you enter in the Text field defines the name of the menu item. You don't have to enter anything in the Menu Item field; that information is automatically generated by what you type in the Text field.

3. In the When selected, go to URL field, either enter a URL for a link or use the Browse button to navigate to and select a file on your site (**Figure 61b**).

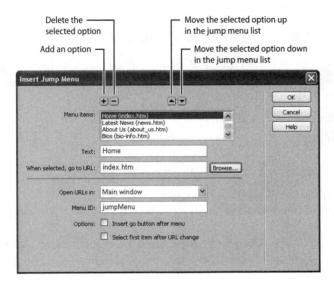

Figure 61b Defining a jump menu link.

4. Define additional jump menu options by clicking the "+" button in the dialog and entering new text and URL. Repeat to enter as many jump menu options as you need. Delete an item from the jump menu by selecting it and clicking the "–" button.

5. To change the order of an item in the jump menu list, select the item and use the Up and Down arrow buttons in the dialog to move the selected item up or down in the list.

6. After you define all the links in the jump menu, click OK to generate the menu. Test the menu in a browser (you can't test it in the Dreamweaver Document window because the jump menu works with JavaScript in a browser).

To edit an existing jump menu, you need to open the behavior that Dreamweaver created to control the jump menu. View the Behaviors panel (choose Window > Behaviors). Click the jump menu to select it. As you do, you will see Jump Menu listed in the second column of the Behaviors panel. Double-click it to reopen the Jump Menu dialog and edit the jump menu (**Figure 61c**).

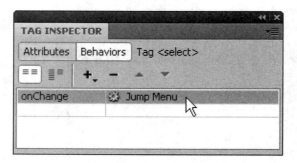

Figure 61c Opening the Jump Menu dialog by double-clicking Jump Menu in the Behaviors panel.

The Jump Menu dialog looks just like the Insert Jump Menu dialog, and you can add, remove, or move menu items or change menu options in this dialog.

#62 Embedding Forms Linked to Server Databases

Many online services provide you with server-side databases and scripts, and these services often host online databases and scripts as well (or else they tell you how to copy them to your server). For example, there are services that allow you to host a mailing list at their server. They provide you with HTML that you copy into your Web page. That HTML contains the coding for the form, as well as a connection to a script at a server that manages the data put into the form.

One of the most popular, easy-to-use, reliable, and professional online form-and-script services is the FreeFind search engine service (www.freefind.com). FreeFind indexes your site (compiles a list of all words in your site in a database) and provides you with a form that visitors can enter search criteria into (**Figure 62a**).

Figure 62a A FreeFind search box; all code and server management is provided by FreeFind.

Follow these steps to place a FreeFind search field on an open Dreamweaver Web page. You can also use them as a model for using similar services.

1. Go to www.freefind.com and enter your email address and your site's URL (at an online server). Click the Instant Signup button. FreeFind emails you a password, a login, and a link to the FreeFind control center. Follow the link, log in, and then click the link for a free search field (or you can choose one of the more elaborate, ad-free pay options).

2. Click the Build Index tab in the FreeFind control center, and then click the Index Now link. FreeFind builds a database at the FreeFind server of all the words in your Web site.

3. Click the HTML tab and choose one of the four available types of search field forms you can use (the options are Site Search Only, Site and Web Search, Web Search Only, or Text Links).

(continued on next page)

Helpful CGI Scripts, Forms, and Hosting Services

In addition to the FreeFind search service, there are a few other useful sources for scripts and hosting to manage form data. These sites provide various sets of available forms and scripts that collect Web statistics, collect feedback, manage message boards, generate survey polls, allow guestbook listings, and store and manage email lists.

- www.thefreecountry.com
- www.cgispy.com
- www.sitegadgets.com
- http://cgi.resourceindex.com

You can find online database and script services by searching for "CGI scripts." CGI stands for Common Gateway Interface and is the protocol (system) that is used (with options for various programming languages) to manage form input.

Can't See Your Form in Dreamweaver?

Normally, forms display in the Document window (in Design view) as red lines. This border is invisible in a browser. Dreamweaver displays the borders of forms as a highly helpful tool so that you can make sure all your form fields are inside your form. If they're not inside the form, they won't work.

Displaying form outlines is a default option that you can turn off. If you don't see the dashed red line indicating the form, turn on this option by choosing View > Visual Aids > Invisible Elements. With Invisible Elements selected in this submenu, you'll be able to see your form.

4. Select all the HTML for the search field you selected, and choose Edit > Copy from your browser menu.

5. Back in Dreamweaver, click in the Document window to set the place where the search field will be inserted. Then choose View > Code to switch to Code view. Don't worry about any of the code you see—your cursor is in the spot you clicked in Design view. Choose Edit > Paste to place the HTML code and switch back to Design view to see the search field (**Figure 62b**).

Note

The form copied from FreeFind includes hidden fields, which are indicated by icons in the form. These fields have information that directs search queries to the index FreeFind prepares for your particular site.

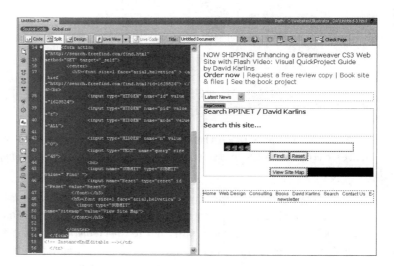

Figure 62b Placing a search field from FreeFind.

Test your search field in a browser. The search field form has fields and buttons. You can reformat the fields and buttons using the techniques for defining form and form field attributes covered in the rest of this chapter. In other words, you can customize the way this form looks—you just can't delete any of the form fields. Other techniques in this chapter cover how customization works, so you can customize forms you get from CGI hosts.

#63 Defining a Form in Dreamweaver

Form data is collected using different kinds of form fields. Text is entered into text boxes or text areas. Options can be selected from sets of radio buttons. Data can be uploaded using file fields. And forms are submitted (or cleared) using Submit (or Reset) buttons.

None of these form *fields*, however, works without a *form*. It's important to be conscious of this. Many of my students get frustrated trying to figure out why their sets of form fields aren't doing anything when the problem is that those form fields are not nested inside a form.

Also, a page can have more than one form. That's often not a good idea from a design standpoint, but you can imagine situations in which you might give visitors a choice of different forms to fill out.

To create a form in an open Web page in Dreamweaver, simply click to place the location of the form and choose Insert > Form > Form. The form displays as a dashed red box. The Property inspector displays the form name.

Make sure you have clicked *inside the form* before you add any form fields (**Figure 63a**)!

Accessible Forms

Forms can be a big challenge for visitors with disabilities. Form accessibility issues include making it easy for disabled visitors (who, for example, cannot use a mouse) to move from field to field in a form and to easily select form fields. Dreamweaver CS4 promotes accessibility in many ways, including form design. If you enable accessibility preferences for form design, Dreamweaver prompts you to enter accessibility features for each form field as you place it in the form.

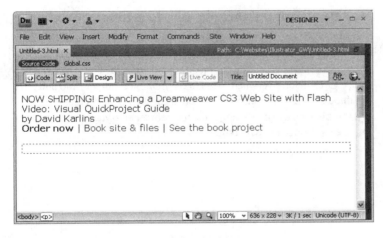

Figure 63a A form placed on a page in Dreamweaver.

To activate prompts for accessibility options in forms, choose Edit > Preferences (Windows) or Dreamweaver > Preferences (Mac) and select

What Are Image Fields?

Image fields are images in a form. They are sometimes used to create customized Submit or Reset buttons, but doing that takes scripting that is not directly available in Dreamweaver.

If you want to place an image field, choose Insert > Form > Image Field. When you do, the Select Image Source dialog opens, and you can navigate to and choose an image to insert into the form.

the Accessibility category. Select the Form objects check box if it is not already selected (**Figure 63b**).

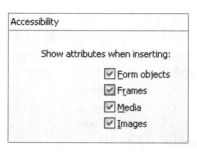

Figure 63b Activating prompts for accessibility options when designing forms in the Accessibility category of the Dreamweaver CS4 Preferences dialog.

With form accessibility options activated, Dreamweaver prompts you with the Input Tag Accessibility Attributes dialog when you insert a form field into a form. The accessibility options allow visitors to fill out the form without using a mouse, or if they are relying on reader software, to have an identifying label read to them.

How Many Characters Are Too Many for a Form?

Some thought needs to go into how many characters you elect to allow in a comment field. My friendly HMO, for instance, allows for something like 25 characters or fewer to describe my medical condition, providing a nice way to raise my frustration level when I need to communicate with the HMO and can't get through by phone! I can only hope other constraints are set more reasonably. There is a point to preventing someone from sending you his or her upcoming screenplay in a comment box.

#64 Defining a Form Fieldset

A fieldset is a design tool used to draw boxes around sections of a form. Fieldsets are particularly useful if you have a long form. Long forms tend to be intimidating or confusing, but by breaking groups of fields into boxed fieldsets, you can make your form more inviting and less overwhelming.

You can also use fieldsets to emphasize a set of fields in a form. For example, if there is some information that is required or that you particularly want to collect, you can enclose that group of fields in a fieldset (**Figure 64a**).

I will review this book at:
I will post or publish a review of this book at:
☐ Amazon.com
☐ A web site or blog:
☐ A print publication :
☐ Other:

Figure 64a A group of fields set off in a form by a fieldset.

To place a fieldset in a form, first make sure your cursor is inside the form. You don't need to worry, initially, about the placement of the form *fields* you want to enclose in the fieldset. You can copy and paste them into the fieldset after you create it. Or, you can click and drag to select the fields you want to include in the fieldset, and then create the fieldset—that way, the fields are automatically enclosed in the fieldset.

With your cursor inside a form, choose Insert > Form > Fieldset (**Figure 64b**).

Figure 64b Defining a fieldset for selected fields in a form.

Fieldsets Are for Design Purposes

Don't get overly confused about the role of fieldsets. They do not affect how a form collects and processes input. And they are not the same as creating a new form. Each form collects a set of data and sends it somewhere—usually to a server database where it is processed. Separate forms can send data to separate databases. Fieldsets, on the other hand, simply draw boxes around sections of a single form to help organize form content and make it more accessible to users.

The Fieldset dialog appears. In the Legend box, type a name that will appear at the top-left corner of the fieldset. This is the label that visitors will read when they see the form in their browsers (**Figure 64c**).

Figure 64c Assigning a legend to a fieldset.

Tip

You can edit a fieldset legend right in the Document window. There is no need (and no way) to reopen the Fieldset dialog; just type right over the existing fieldset label to change it.

#65 Placing Text Fields and Text Areas

Text fields are used to collect all kinds of information in a form. Email addresses, phone numbers, purchase prices, zip codes, names, and a wide variety of other data can be entered into text fields.

Text *fields* collect a single line of text. Text *areas* can collect multiple lines of text. Text areas are used to collect comments, descriptions (like descriptions of problems for online service forms), guestbook entries, and other text that requires more than one line.

To place a text field or a text area in a form, follow these steps:

1. With your cursor inside an existing form, choose Insert > Form > Text Field or Insert > Form > Text Area.

2. After you place the text field, you can define the field attributes in the Property inspector (**Figure 65**). In the TextField field, enter a name that will help you remember the content of the field. In the Char width field, enter the number of characters that will display on a single line in a browser as a visitor enters data.

Figure 65 Defining a one-line text field.

3. In the Max chars field, you can enter the maximum number of characters that can be entered into the field.

4. In the Init val field, enter text that will appear in the field in a browser before any user interaction. Sometimes (but not always) form designers will include text like "your email goes here" in a field. Visitors then replace that content with their own entry.

5. In the Type options, choose Single line for a text field and Multiline for a text area. If you choose Multiline, the Num Lines field appears in the Property inspector. Enter the number of lines that will display in the form (you cannot define a limit for the number of characters that are entered).

(continued on next page)

Text Field Accessibility

If you have enabled accessibility options, you'll be prompted to enter a label for each text field you define. Labels are read out loud by reader software and make it easy for visitors to identify fields and enter content.

6. Enable the Password option to display content entered into the field as asterisks.

7. You can use the Class pop-up menu to attach a CSS Class style to the field.

Tip

As you define text field or text area attributes in the Property inspector, they display in the Document window.

#66 Placing Check Boxes

You can place any number of check boxes in a form. Check boxes provide two options for visitors: Checked or Unchecked. And you can define a default state for a check box as either checked or unchecked.

To place a check box in a form, follow these steps:

1. With your cursor inside an existing form, choose Insert > Form > Checkbox.

2. After you place the check box, if you did not generate a label, you need to enter some text in the form (normally to the right of the check box) that identifies what is being selected when a visitor selects the check box.

3. In the Property inspector, enter a name for the check box in the Check-box name field. In the Checked value field, enter a value to go with the check box name. For example, if the check box asks if a user wants to be contacted, the check box name might be "contact" and the checked value might be "yes."

4. Select one of the Initial state options to define whether the default state of the check box is Checked or Unchecked (**Figure 66**).

Figure 66 Defining a check box.

Attaching Class Styles to Text Fields

You can use the Class pop-up in the Property inspector to attach a CSS Class style to any field. However, this is sometimes especially handy for text (or text area) fields because you can format the text that a user enters into the form. See Chapter 6, #38, "Create Class CSS Formatting Rules for Text," for a discussion on how to create and apply Custom class styles.

Accessible Check Boxes

If you have enabled accessibility options, you'll be prompted to enter them—including a label—before defining the field. See #63, "Defining a Form in Dreamweaver," for an explanation. Do enter a label (check boxes need text to tell visitors what they are checking, and generated labels do this well); the label will display to the left or right of the check box.

Checkbox Protocol

There are different styles and systems for identifying and collecting data in check boxes. If you are designing a form in conjunction with a database programmer, check with that programmer on how to manage this.

#**67** Placing Radio Buttons

Radio buttons differ from check boxes in that they are always organized in groups. You never have a single radio button—if you are asking a question for which a user can supply no, one, or several answers, use check boxes. The purpose of radio buttons is to compel a user to choose *one* from a *group* of options.

To create a radio button group, follow these steps:

1. With your cursor inside an existing form, choose Insert > Form > Radio Group. The Radio Group dialog appears (**Figure 67**).

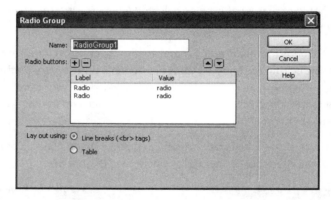

Figure 67 Defining a group of radio buttons.

2. In the Name field, enter a name that indicates *to you* the nature of the group of options. For example, if you are inquiring as to a type of shipping (Overnight, Two-day, Ground, etc.), you might call your group "Shipping_options."

3. In the Radio buttons area of the dialog, click the Label column. In the first row enter a label that will appear for visitors. Next to that label, in the Value column, enter the data that will be sent with the form. For example, a label might read "Two-day shipping" to make clear to a user what he or she is selecting. But the value sent to your shipping department might be "TD-002"—an internal code that tells those in the department how to handle and bill shipping.

4. In the second row, enter another label and value. Use the "+" button to add more rows of labels and values and the "–" button to delete a

selected row. Use the Up and Down arrow buttons to move selected rows up or down in the list of radio buttons.

5. In the Lay out using area, choose either the Line breaks radio button (for separated rows) or Table radio button (for rows designed in a table).

6. After you define the radio button options, click OK in the dialog to generate the radio button group.

After you generate a radio button group, you can edit (or delete) radio buttons individually. If you want to add a radio button, you can copy and paste an existing one from the group and, in the Property inspector, change the Checked value (but not the Radio Button) content.

Radio Button Group Names

Why don't you change the Radio Button information when you edit radio buttons? Because the Radio Button value defines the *group*. The values of individual radio buttons within a group can change, but the group name must be the same for all buttons in the group. You can test your radio button group in a browser; if you choose one option from within the group, all other options should become deselected. If that doesn't happen, you haven't assigned the exact same group name (in the Radio Button field in the Property inspector) to each radio button.

Because radio buttons are organized into groups, they are a little more complicated to define than other form fields. And because Dreamweaver is the ultimate Web design program, it includes a dialog (Radio Group) that manages the whole process of defining a radio button group easily.

Radio Buttons Get Generated with Labels

Among the advantages of using Dreamweaver's Label dialog is that accessible labels are generated along with the radio button group and individual radio button values. There is no need for a distinct process of defining accessibility options for radio button groups if you use Dreamweaver's radio button group feature.

#68 Placing Lists/Menus and File Fields

Menus and file fields are two different types of fields that can be placed in forms. Menus allow visitors to choose from a list of items. File fields allow users to upload files when they submit a form. In this how-to, you'll explore both types of fields. (Consider this two how-tos for the price of one—I had to sneak them both into the same how-to to keep the book at an even 100 how-tos!)

Menus (sometimes called pop-up menus) allow visitors to choose one option from a pop-up menu. The main difference between menus and list menus is that list menus allow users to select more than one choice from a list, whereas regular menus restrict users to choosing just one item. List menus are usually a confusing way to collect data and are rarely used.

To create a menu, follow these steps:

1. With your cursor inside an existing form, choose Insert > Form > List/Menu. You use this menu option to create *either* a menu or a list menu. Later, you will decide whether to make your menu a list menu or a regular menu.

2. To create a list for the menu, click the List Values button in the Property inspector. The List Values dialog appears. In the Item Label column, enter the text that will display in the menu (for example, "Alaska"). In the Value column, enter the value that will be collected and sent in the form (such as "AK"). Use the "+" button to add new items to the list and the "–" button to delete selected items. After you define the list, click OK (**Figure 68a**).

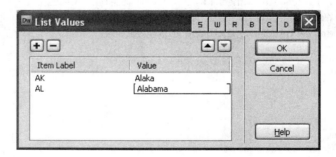

Figure 68a Defining a list/menu.

3. After you generate a menu (or list), use the Property inspector to define additional features. If you click the List option button in the Type area of the Property inspector, you can convert the menu into a list menu. And if you choose the List option, you can click the Allow Multiple check box in the Options area of the Property inspector to allow users to choose more than one option from the menu. List menus can also display more than one option at a time in the drop-down menu.

4. You can add, delete, or edit actual menu (or list) items by clicking the List Values button in the Property inspector. This will open the List Values dialog where you can edit or change the order of menu (or list) options. You can change the initially selected option in the Property inspector by clicking an option in the Initially selected area (**Figure 68b**). You can assign a CSS style using the Class pop-up menu.

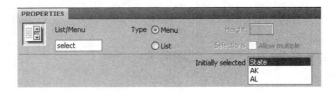

Figure 68b Choosing an Initially selected option for a pop-up menu.

Note
The Property inspector must be expanded to see the Initially selected option.

File field forms allow visitors to attach files from their own computers to the form and send them along with the form. You can allow visitors to attach files to the form submission by inserting a File field in a form. Choose Insert > Form > File Field. You can define character width in the Property inspector. A Browse button appears next to the field that the user can use to navigate to and select a file to upload.

Don't Limit Filename Sizes

Don't constrain the number of characters that visitors can use to define an uploaded file by entering a value in the Max chars field in the Property inspector. There is no point to setting a limit on the number of characters in an uploaded file's name.

#**69** Using Hidden Fields

Hidden fields send information to a server that is not entered by the visitor filling out the online form. Hidden fields can be used to identify things like the page from which a form was sent.

Normally, you won't be creating hidden fields. It's more likely that they will be included in the HTML for a form that you download, connected to an existing server script. For instance, the form provided by FreeFind to link to a search index database at its server includes several hidden fields (**Figure 69**).

Figure 69 Examining hidden field values in Code view.

If you do need to create a hidden field in a form, choose Insert > Form > Hidden Field. The field, of course, does not display in the form; it appears only as an icon in the Document window. Enter a name for the field in the HiddenField field in the Property inspector and enter a value in the Value field.

#**70** Placing Form Buttons

For form content to be sent to a server, there must be a Submit button in the form. Submit buttons are usually matched with a Reset button. The Reset button clears any data entered into the form and allows the user to start fresh.

To place a button in a form, choose Insert > Form > Button. Use the Property inspector to define the button as a Submit or Reset button. In the Action area of the Property inspector, choose the Submit form or Reset form radio button (**Figure 70a**).

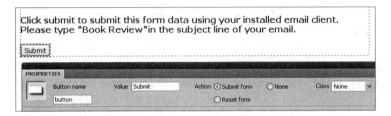

Figure 70a Defining a Submit button.

You can define custom labels for either the Submit or Reset button by entering text in the Value field for either button. Don't get too fancy; visitors are used to seeing buttons that display something like Submit or Reset. But if you enter different text in the Value field, that text will display in browsers and can be previewed in the Document window (**Figure 70b**).

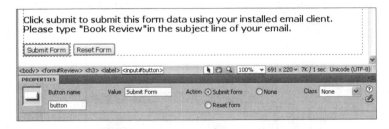

Figure 70b Creating a custom label for a Submit button.

#71 Defining Form Actions

Form actions define how the data in a form is sent to a database on a server. Form actions are defined in the Property inspector with the *form*—not any specific form field—selected.

Tip
To select a form, click the dashed red line defining the form border. Or, click the <form> tag in the tag selector area on the bottom of the Document window.

The three important fields in the Property inspector for a form are the Action, Method, and Enctype fields. What you enter into these fields is determined by how the programmer (who set up the script and database to which the form data is being sent) configured the database and scripts at the server. Normally, Method is usually set to POST but can sometimes be set to GET; this again depends on how data is transferred to the server and is defined by how the server is configured. The Action field contains the URL of the Web page at the server that has the script that will manage the data.

Enctype, short for "encryption type," is sometimes used to define how characters are interpreted and formatted. Your server administrator will tell you what, if any, enctype coding is required for forms to be processed by your server.

Since form actions are determined by the settings at your server, the information you enter into the Property inspector is provided by your server administrator. In the case of forms designed to match server scripts, those forms normally come with Action settings defined (**Figure 71a**).

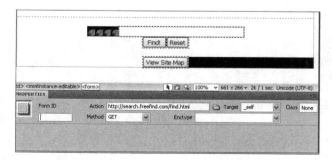

Figure 71a Inspecting form action settings provided by a server administrator—in this case the FreeFind search engine.

Don't Mess with Hidden Fields in Imported Forms

If a CGI script provider gives you HTML to create a form to send data to a server, the provider will likely include hidden fields. These hidden fields define how the data is processed at the server. It's best if you don't edit or delete them.

Sending Form Content via Email— Pro and Con

The easiest way to collect form content is to have the content sent to an email address. This is the model used in this technique. The advantage is that it requires no scripting on your part. The downside is that it requires the person submitting the form to have an installed email client on his or her system. Although many users who have Internet access on their system have an email client as well, people using public computers at schools or libraries will not have access to email clients. For some applications, this is a problem.

Collecting Data in Forms

If you want to collect data in a form and have it sent to an email address, you can do this easily without having to work with additional server configuration or scripts. In the Action field, type mailto:*<your email address>*. From the Method pop-up menu, choose POST. In the Enctype field, type text/plain (**Figure 71b**).

Figure 71b Defining an action that will send form content to an email address—in this case, mine!

CHAPTER ELEVEN

Defining Spry Validation Widgets

Adobe has implanted several Spry tools in Dreamweaver CS4 that make it easy to define forms with attached validation scripts. These scripts test form content before it is submitted to make sure certain rules are met; specifically in the case of the new Spry form fields, they require that a visitor fill in a form field before submitting the form.

For example, if you want to require that visitors fill in the E-mail Address field in a form before they submit it, you can place a Spry Validation Text Field in your form. The four how-tos in this chapter explain how to use these Spry validation widgets.

All Spry validation widgets generate JavaScript to allow a form field to test input before processing the form. They also generate new CSS files that contain the formatting that defines the color, background color, text format, and so on for the form field and for form field input.

#72 Validating Text Field Input

Many times you will want to test content entered into a text field before you allow a visitor to submit the form. For example, you might require a visitor to enter his or her name before submitting a form. In that case, the validation test would be that a visitor could not leave the Name field blank before submitting it. The Spry Validation Text Field widget can detect a blank field and alert the person filling out the form that a name is required before the form can be submitted.

Or, you might want to test content entered into a text field even beyond determining whether or not the field was left blank. If, for example, you are collecting a zip code from the visitor, you can test to see if the data entered into the zip code field actually is a five- (or nine-) digit zip code. You can use the Spry Validation Text Field widget to verify that the data submitted in the form field conforms to the criteria you define, and again, force people to provide data that at least looks like a zip code before the form can be submitted.

To place a Spry Validation Text Field widget in a form, follow these steps:

1. *Within a form,* select Insert > Spry > Spry Validation Text Field.

2. A text field appears in your form. With the new text field selected, the Spry text field options are displayed in the Property inspector.

3. In the Spry TextField box in the Property inspector, enter a field name with no spaces or special characters (use alphanumeric characters). The field name is used to process data and is not displayed in a browser.

4. By default, the Required check box is selected in the Property inspector. Leave this check box selected to make the text field a required field.

5. If you want to test data entered into the text field to meet validation criteria (for instance, the data must be in the form of an email address, a zip code, a URL, or a phone number), select one of those options from the Type pop-up menu in the Property inspector (**Figure 72a**).

Figure 72a Choosing Email Address as the validation type.

Defining Spry Validation Widgets

6. Many of the preset validation types include additional options. For example, if you chose to test input for zip codes, you can test for five-digit (US-5), nine-digit (US-9), British (UK), or Canadian (Canada) format. The Format pop-up menu displays these options (**Figure 72b**).

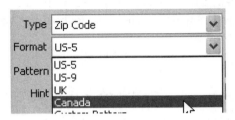

Figure 72b Selecting from zip code testing options.

7. The Enforce Pattern check box makes it impossible for users to enter characters that do not conform to the validation rule. For example, if you define validation rules for a U.S. zip code and a user tries to enter a letter (like A), that character will not appear in the field.

8. Use the Hint box in the Property inspector to provide initial content in the text field (for instance, you might use "youremail@email.com" to suggest to users that they need to enter a complete email address).

9. Choose when to validate the field entry from the set of Validate on check boxes. Use Blur to validate when a user clicks outside the text field. Select Change to validate as the user changes text inside the text field. Choosing Submit validates when the user clicks the Submit button in the form.

10. Many of the preset validation types include rules of how many characters will be allowed and/or maximum and minimum values. For example, the five-digit zip code validation type will only accept five numbers.

11. The Preview States pop-up menu in the Property inspector just defines what state is displayed in the Document window in Dreamweaver. The state that displays in a browser depends on whether or not the user conforms to or breaks the validation rules.

12. You can edit Spry validation rules at any time by selecting the turquoise Spry TextField label and changing values in the Property inspector.

Create Your Own Validation Rules

You can create your own validation rules for text boxes by choosing Integer (number) from the Type pop-up menu in the Property inspector, and then defining a maximum (Max chars) and/or minimum (Min chars) number of characters, and a maximum (Max value) and/or minimum (Min value) value for numbers entered into the field.

Spry Validation Text Field Widgets Don't Verify Actual Data

To be clear: None of the Spry Validation Text Field widgets actually looks up data and verifies that it is accurate. But the widgets do verify that at least the correct form of data has been submitted, eliminating forms that are sent to your server that don't have required information fields filled in.

#73 Validating Text Area Input

Text area fields are used almost exclusively for comments. And comments in this digital age are one of the more available ways that customers, clients, students, patients, and people in general communicate with organizations and businesses.

If you place a text area field in a form, you might well want to use the Spry Validation Textarea widget to define a few rules for how much content can be entered into the field.

To place a Spry Validation Textarea widget in a form, follow these steps:

1. *Within a form,* select Insert > Spry > Spry Validation Textarea.

2. A text area appears in your form. With the new text field selected, the Spry text field options are displayed in the Property inspector.

3. In the Spry Textarea box in the Property inspector, enter a field name with no spaces or special characters (use alphanumeric characters). The field name is used to process data and is not displayed in a browser.

4. By default, the Required check box is selected in the Property inspector. Leave this check box selected if you want to make the text area a required field.

5. Use the Hint box in the Property inspector to provide "hint" content in the text field (for instance, you might have text like "your comment here" or "comment required") (**Figure 73**).

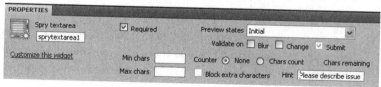

Figure 73 Defining hint content for a comment field.

Why Validate Textarea Input?

You can use the Spry Validation Textarea widget to make a text area field required. For example, if customers are asked to describe what kind of service their laptops need, you might want to insist that they describe their problem before submitting a request for service.

Area Type Accessibility

If you have accessibility prompts turned on, you will be prompted to enter accessibility attributes for the text field, like an accessible label.

6. Choose when to validate the field entry from the set of Validate on check boxes. Use Blur to validate when a user clicks outside the text field. Select Change to validate as the user changes text inside the text field. Choosing Submit validates when the user clicks the Submit button in the form.

7. Enter values in the Max chars and/or Min chars boxes in the Property inspector to constrain the number of characters that can be entered into the field.

8. If you define a maximum number of characters in the Textarea field, you can use the Counter options to define whether to display a count of used or remaining characters.

9. The Preview States pop-up menu in the Property inspector just defines what state is displayed in the Document window in Dreamweaver. The state that displays in a browser depends on whether or not the user conforms to or breaks the validation rules.

You can edit Spry validation rules at any time by selecting the turquoise Spry Textarea label and changing values in the Property inspector.

#**74** Validating Checkbox Input

Sometimes a check box provides an option that a user can either choose or not. Do you want to receive unsolicited email? Do you have a discount code? Did you hear about this Web site from a friend? In all these cases, a form designer will likely allow the user to select, or not, any or all of the check boxes.

In other cases, clicking a check box is mandatory to submit a form. Required check boxes are used to verify that a visitor has read a license agreement before downloading software or that a visitor agrees to set terms before reading site content. In situations like these, you can use a Spry Validation Checkbox widget to require that a visitor select a check box before submitting a form.

To insert a Spry Validation Checkbox *in an existing form*, follow these steps:

1. With your cursor in a form, select Insert > Spry > Spry Validation Checkbox.

   ### Note
   If you have accessibility prompts turned on, you will be prompted to enter accessibility attributes for the text field. Form field accessibility attributes are explained in #63, "Defining a Form in Dreamweaver." You can enter accessibility attributes, or not. Click OK to insert the form field.

2. The Required option is selected in the Property inspector. This is the main point of using this widget, and it is likely you will not need to define any other options. However, you can define when to validate the field entry using the set of three different Validate on check boxes. Use Blur to validate when a user clicks outside the text field.

Select Change to validate as the user changes text inside the text field. Submit is always selected and validates when the user clicks the Submit button in the form (**Figure 74**).

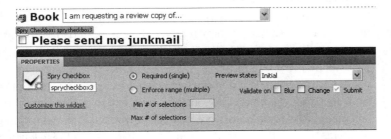

Figure 74 Defining validation for a check box triggered by a user clicking the Submit button.

3. The Preview States pop-up menu in the Property inspector just defines what state is displayed in the Document window in Dreamweaver. The state that displays in a browser depends on whether or not the user conforms to or breaks the validation rules.

4. You can edit Spry validation rules at any time by selecting the turquoise Spry Checkbox label and changing settings in the Property inspector.

Notice that the Property inspector for a Spry check box includes an Enforce Range (Multiple) option. This allows you to define a minimum number of check boxes that must be selected before the form can be submitted.

#75 Validating Menu Input

Spry Validation Select widgets are used to create validation rules for pop-up menus. (Dreamweaver uses the term "select menus" for what most folks refer to as pop-up menus or popups). Spry Validation Select widgets are used to force users to make a selection from a pop-up menu. For example, if the pop-up menu lists a set of geographical regions and you need to know what geographical region a client is located in, you might make it a requirement that before submitting a form the client provides his or her location.

Creating a Spry Validation Select widget is a two-part process. Unlike the other Spry validation widgets surveyed in this chapter, the Spry Validation Select widget does not generate a working form field; it only generates the validation script. So, you need to generate the validation widget *and* create a pop-up menu with options.

Defining labels and values for (pop-up) menus is covered in #68, "Placing Lists/Menus and File Fields," in Chapter 10. Here, I'll walk you through generating a Spry Validation Select widget that provides a validation script for a menu.

To generate a Spry Validation Select widget, click in a form and choose Insert > Spry > Spry Validation Select. An empty menu is generated. You can populate the menu after you define the validation rules in the Property inspector.

The unique validation option for a menu is that you can force visitors to choose an option from the menu. You can also constrain the selected option to a menu option with a value. Let's start with the basic option: By default, Spry Validation Select scripts create a required form. If a user doesn't select an option from the menu, he or she will be unable to submit the form (**Figure 75a**).

Figure 75a The Property inspector displays the default validation rule for Spry Validation Select widgets—blank values are not allowed.

In addition to screening for blank value submissions, you can also define a value (besides blank) that you assign to menu options that are not accepted. For instance, if you are collecting data in the menu about where someone bought your product before you provide support for his or her purchase, you might define a form that would not accept menu selections like "I don't know" or "I stole it!" In that case, you would define a value (like "1," for instance) for all menu options that you will not accept and enter that value in the Invalid value field, along with selecting the Invalid value check box (**Figure 75b**).

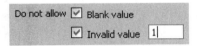

Figure 75b Defining an invalid value of 1.

After you attach a validation script to a menu, click the *menu field* (as opposed to the turquoise validation script label) in the Dreamweaver Document window. In the List/Menu Property inspector, click the List Values button to open the List Values dialog. Here, you enter labels and values for your menu.

CHAPTER TWELVE

Embedding Media

In this chapter, I'll walk you through the process of adding Flash Video (both traditional playable Flash SWF files and the newer and more widely used FLV format), Windows Media, and QuickTime files to your Dreamweaver CS4 Web pages.

You can add digital media to your site quickly and easily. This book cannot explore the whole fascinating and wide-ranging scope of software tools and techniques involved in generating video or audio files. But almost every computer shipped these days comes with at least a basic program for editing and producing digital audio and video files you create with your digital video camera, audio recording device, or whatever level of media production tools is available to you.

#76 Embedding Flash Files

When you embed a Flash (SWF) file or a Flash Video file in a Web page in Dreamweaver, you can adjust the size of the movie, define the size and color of a background behind the movie, and even adjust features like whether or not the movie plays automatically when the page in which it is inserted opens or if a visitor has to click a Play button to watch the movie.

Despite the similar-sounding names, Flash movies (SWF files) and Flash Video (FLV files) are different things. Flash movies, often referred to as SWFs (often pronounced "swiffs"), present animated and interactive content online, and are created with Adobe's Flash authoring tool. The SWF format is also sometimes used to display digital artwork online.

To insert a SWF file into an open Web page, choose Insert > Media > SWF. If you have not saved the open document, Dreamweaver will prompt you to do so.

After you choose Insert > Media > SWF, the Select File dialog appears. Navigate to a SWF file, and click OK.

If you have selected accessibility prompts for SWF files in the Preferences dialog, you'll be prompted to enter a title for your SWF video (**Figure 76a**).

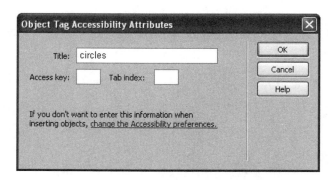

Figure 76a Entering a title to make a SWF file more accessible.

When you embed a SWF file in a Web page, the movie appears as a gray box. When selected, the Property inspector for the movie is active (**Figure 76b**).

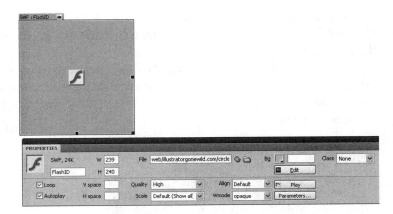

Figure 76b The Property inspector for a SWF movie.

How Accessible Are Flash Movies?

Flash files require the Adobe Flash Player, which is installed on a large percentage of computers and is also available as a free download (via www.adobe.com).

- Use the Loop and AutoPlay check boxes to enable (or disable) looping (repeating) or autoplay (the animation plays when a page is loaded).

- The V Space and H Space fields allow you to define vertical (V) or horizontal (H) spacing between the Flash movie and other objects on the page.

- The Quality pop-up menu allows you to compress the Flash file (choose Low) for faster downloading and lower quality.

- In the Scale pop-up menu, the Default setting maintains the original height-to-width ratio of the original animation (that is, it prevents the animation from being distorted) when the Flash object is resized. The Exact Fit option in the Scale pop-up menu, on the other hand, allows you to stretch the animation horizontally or vertically if you change the original height and/or width.

- The Align pop-up menu is used to align the Flash object left or right, so text flows around the animation.

- The Bg pop-up menu is used to define a background color. The background color is active if you resize the Flash object and maintain the height-to-width aspect ratio by choosing the Default setting in the Scale field.

- The Reset size button restores the Flash object to its original size. The Edit button opens Flash (if you have it installed) to edit the Flash object.

- The Play button displays the Flash object in the Document window. Toggling to Stop displays the editable gray box.

#77 Inserting Flash Video (FLV) and Player Skins

Adobe is very successfully promoting the FLV format as a kind of "universal" video format that transcends other competing media formats. This is the video format used at YouTube.

Dreamweaver CS4 allows you to embed movies that have been saved to the FLV format, and then choose from a nice little set of player controls that display in a browser window to make it easy for visitors to control the movie (**Figure 77a**).

How Do You Create FLVs?

The Flash Video Encoder (renamed the Adobe Video Encoder in CS4) transforms Windows Media or QuickTime videos into FLV format. For a complete, detailed, step-by-step guide to editing and generating FLVs, and embedding FLV files in a Dreamweaver Web site, see *Enhancing a Dreamweaver CS3 Web Site with Flash Video: Visual QuickProject Guide* (Peachpit, 2008) by David Karlins.

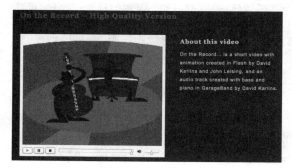

Figure 77a Watching an FLV file.

To embed an FLV file, follow these steps:

1. Choose Insert > Media > FLV. The Insert FLV dialog opens. Use the Browse button to navigate to an FLV file (or enter the URL of a file on the Internet) in the URL field. Unless you are working with a special streaming server (and your server administrator will know this information), choose Progressive Download Video from the Video type pop-up menu.

2. Click the Detect Size button in the dialog to detect the size of the video. Keep the Constrain check box selected since it is unlikely that you will want to distort the height-to-width ratio of the video. You can enter a new value in either the Width or Height field to resize the video. If you selected the Constrain check box, the nonedited dimension will automatically adjust to keep the height-to-width ratio of the video the same as the original (**Figure 77b**).

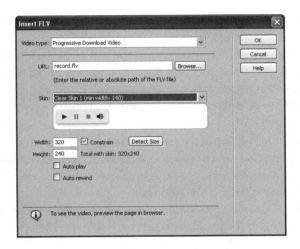

Figure 77b Embedding a Flash Video file with detected size.

3. After detecting the video size, you can use the Skin pop-up menu to select a player control set. Note that player controls require various sizes of videos, which is why you detected the video size in step 2 first (**Figure 77c**).

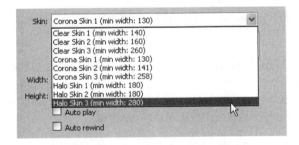

Figure 77c Choosing a Flash Player skin for an FLV video.

4. You can enable Auto play or Auto rewind, or Prompt users to download Flash Player features if necessary using the check boxes in the dialog. If you elect to prompt users to download the Flash Player, you can accept or edit the text message that displays.

Many Flash Video parameters you set when you embed the video can be edited in the Property inspector.

#**78** Embedding QuickTime Media

Following are a few useful parameters for controlling the display of QuickTime movies:

- The BGCOLOR parameter defines the background color. Enter standard colors (like red, blue, green, black) or hexadecimal color values.

- The SCALE parameter enlarges a video by making the resolution more grainy. Setting scale value to 2, for example, doubles the size of the video display without affecting the number of pixels.

- The AUTOPLAY parameter can be set to true (the video plays when the page opens) or false.

- The VOLUME parameter defines the default volume for the video when it plays on a scale of 1 (quiet) to 10 (loud).

QuickTime movies can be easily embedded in Dreamweaver pages. And you can easily reset the size at which QuickTime movies will display. However, Dreamweaver does not provide easy-to-use sets of controllers for QuickTime movies like it does for Flash Video. Features like background color, autoplay, and scale (enlargement of a video by displaying it at a lower resolution) are all defined with parameters that must be entered manually.

To embed a QuickTime movie, choose Insert > Media > Plugin. The all-purpose Select File dialog (which is used for all types of plug-ins, not just QuickTime files) opens. Navigate to the QuickTime (MOV) file you want to insert, and click Choose (Mac) or OK (Windows).

The embedded QuickTime movie appears as a very minimalist 32-pixel square box regardless of the size of the actual movie (**Figure 78a**).

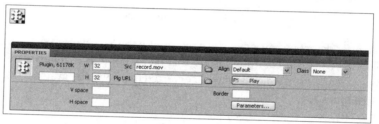

Figure 78a Default dimensions and settings for an embedded QuickTime movie in the Property inspector.

To display the movie at an appropriate size, enter a height and width in the Property inspector. You can also enter vertical (V) or horizontal (H) spacing in the Property inspector. Use the Align pop-up menu to align the movie on the left or right side of the page (**Figure 78b**).

Figure 78b Defining dimensions, spacing, and alignment for a QuickTime movie.

You have to manually enter display parameters into the Parameters section of the Property inspector. Click the Parameters button in the Property inspector to display the Parameters dialog. You can add parameters by clicking the "+" button in the dialog. Enter a parameter in the left column, and enter a value in the right column. After you set parameters, click OK to close the Parameters dialog.

You can preview your QuickTime movie in the Dreamweaver Document window by clicking the Play button in the Property inspector. Or, you can preview a QuickTime video using Live view, but you'll have more reliable preview results if you preview the page with the movie in a Web browser (choose File > Preview in Browser, and then select a browser from the available list if you have more than one).

Downloading the QuickTime Player for Windows

QuickTime audio and video files require the Apple Quick-Time Player (a free download, available at www.apple.com/quicktime). The QuickTime Player *is* installed on all Macs. However, by default, QuickTime Player is not installed on many Windows computers.

Find More QuickTime Parameters

Parameters for embedding QuickTime movies can be found at www.apple.com/quicktime/tutorials/embed2.html.

#79 Embedding Windows Media

Like QuickTime movies, Windows Media files (which can be WMV, AVI, and other file types) can be easily embedded in Dreamweaver. You can also easily reset the size at which Windows Media movies will display. As with QuickTime movies, Dreamweaver does not provide easy-to-use sets of controllers for Windows Media movies.

And, as with QuickTime movies, you need to manually define parameters to control features like autoplay, initial volume, and whether or not a player control displays in the browser with the video.

To embed a Windows Media movie, choose Insert > Media > Plugin. The Select File dialog (used for all types of plug-ins) opens. Navigate to the Windows Media file you want to insert, and click Choose (Mac) or OK (Windows).

The embedded Windows Media movie is placed on the page in a 32-pixel square box regardless of the size of the actual movie. To display the movie at an appropriate size, enter a width and height in the Property inspector. You can also enter vertical (V) or horizontal (H) spacing in the Property inspector. Use the Align pop-up menu to align the movie on the left or right side of the page (**Figure 79a**).

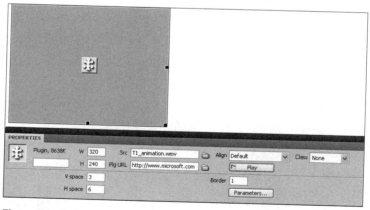

Figure 79a Embedding a Windows Media file.

The best way to see how your Windows Media file will look in a browser is to preview the movie in a browser (choose File > Preview in Browser, and then select a browser from the available list if you have more than one).

To define how the Windows Media file displays and plays in a browser, you enter parameters into the Parameters area of the Property inspector. Click the Parameters button in the Property inspector to display the Parameters dialog. You can add parameters by clicking the "+" button in the dialog. Enter a parameter in the left column, and enter a value in the right column.

Following are a few useful parameters for controlling the display of Windows Media movies:

- The AUTOSTART parameter with the Value set to true plays a movie automatically when the page opens. When the Value is set to false, it does not and requires the visitor to start the movie using a control.

- The DISPLAYBACKCOLOR parameter can have the Value set to false (no background color) or a color (like red, blue, green, or black), or a hexadecimal value.

- The SHOWAUDIOCONTROLS parameter can have the Value set to true (a volume control displays) or false (no control).

After you set parameters, click OK to close the Parameters dialog (**Figure 79b**).

Figure 79b Defining parameters for a Windows Media movie.

Where Do You Find Windows Media Parameters?

There are many versions of Windows Media Player, and they use different parameters. While QuickTime parameters are standardized and managed by Apple, the world of Windows Media is less defined. You can use Google to search for Windows Media parameters, but you'll have to sort through competing and conflicting sets of parameters. The bottom line is that Windows Media video will display in a visitor's browser window in unpredictable ways. Windows Media is almost universally supported, but developers who need tight control over the display of embedded video turn to Flash Video, Real Video, or QuickTime.

CHAPTER THIRTEEN

Adding Effects and Interactivity with Spry

Introduced in Dreamweaver CS3, and with an updated set of features in CS4, Spry widgets provide access to dynamic and interactive elements that until now had to be created in other programs. Spry widgets include menu bars, tabbed panels, accordion effects, collapsible panels, and definable tooltips.

You need to be aware of a few things when you create Spry widgets:

- Documents must be saved before you insert Spry widgets.

- Spry widgets generate lots of CSS styles and JavaScript files, and these files are saved every time you save a page with a Spry widget.

- You control basic features of the Spry widget, like text and links, in the Property inspector. But you format Spry widgets (elements like font, text color, background color, and so on) in the CSS Styles panel by editing the CSS style for the Spry widget.

Managing Spry widgets on a page can get confusing, especially when you have several of them loaded in a page. Before diving into specific Spry widgets, let's quickly go over how you *delete* a Spry widget if you need to.

To select (and then delete) a Spry widget in Design view of the Document window:

1. Click on the border of the widget or the widget label that appears at the top-left corner of the widget when you hover over that spot to select the widget.

2. Press the Delete key to remove the widget from your page.

#80 Creating a Spry Menu Bar

Menu bars, which display submenus when they are hovered over, are a very useful and appealing page element. Menu bars allow several menu options to be accessed from a clean, uncluttered main menu. The interactivity they provide when a visitor hovers over a menu option adds energy and dynamism to your page.

The Spry widget for inserting Menu Bar widgets allows you to generate menu bars with two levels of submenus. That means a user can click on a menu option that will in turn reveal a submenu with a new set of options, choose one of those options, and pick from yet a second submenu.

To generate a Menu Bar widget, you must first save the page into which the Menu Bar widget will be inserted. Then choose Insert > Spry > Spry Menu Bar. The Spry Menu Bar dialog appears, and you can choose between a horizontal or vertical menu bar (**Figure 80a**). OK the Spry Menu Bar dialog to generate the Menu Bar widget.

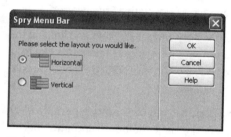

Figure 80a Choosing a horizontal Spry menu bar.

The menu bar that is generated is generic with four menu items (Item 1, Item 2, Item 3, and Item 4). You can customize basic menu bar properties like the display menu name and the link target in the Property inspector.

To edit the content and links for a selected menu bar, choose menu items (initially labeled Item 1, Item 2, etc.) or submenu items (initially labeled Item 1.1, Item 1.2, etc) in the Property inspector.

With an item (or subitem) selected, you can enter text in the active Text field of the Property inspector that will appear in the menu. In the Link box you can enter the link that will open when the item is clicked.

Use the Title box in the Property inspector to enter accessibility text (this text will appear in a browser window when a user hovers over the menu option). Leave the Target box blank to open the link in the same browser window or enter _blank to open the link in a new browser window.

Remember: Save Before You Spry

Before you create any Spry widgets, make sure you save the Web page you are working on. To insert tabbed panels, place your cursor where the tabbed panels will appear (usually at the top of a page) and choose Insert > Spry > Spry Tabbed Panels. By default, a two-tab tabbed panel appears.

What Are the Div Tags for Widgets?

Widget div tag names vary depending on the particular widget and how many of that particular widget you have on a page. But the div tags all begin with "div." followed by the name of the particular widget. For example, the tag for a Collapsible Panel widget begins "div.CollapsiblePanel," and then will vary depending on how many collapsible panels you have on your page.

You can use the "+" and "–" icons above the menu or submenu (or sub-submenu) columns to add or delete new menu items. Use the Move Item Up or Move Item Down icons to change the order of menu items (**Figure 80b**).

Horizontal or Vertical Menu Bars?

Menu Bar widgets can be horizontal or vertical. Vertical menu bars typically are aligned in a frame, table column, or other layout objects (like a div or an AP div) on the left side of the page. Horizontal menu bars are typically aligned on the top of the page and can be placed there without being inserted in a layout object.

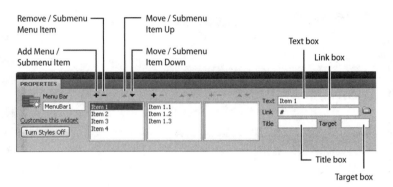

Figure 80b The Property inspector for menu bars.

When you select a Menu Bar widget (or as you create one), you will notice a Turn Styles Off button in the Property inspector. Turning styles off does not affect how the style is rendered in a browser, but it turns off formatting in the Document window (essentially reducing your menu bar to an outline in the Document window). You can adjust the formatting of different menu bar properties of a selected menu bar in the CSS Styles panel.

Some of the CSS Style options control relatively inconspicuous elements of the menu bar, but all of them can be edited in the CSS Styles panel.

What Are All Those Menu Bar Styles About?

Most of the CSS styles that are generated to format your Menu Bar widget define the positioning and size of the menus and submenus that appear when a user hovers over a menu option. The default positioning of these menus is usually fine and does not need to be adjusted. You can customize a very unique menu bar by creating your own links and text, and you can create a distinctive format by customizing text and background colors.

To edit the styles associated with a Menu Bar widget, expand the menu bar style sheet in the CSS Styles panel. This style sheet will be named Spry-MenuBarHorizontal.css, or SpryMenuBarVertical.css if you created a vertical menu bar (**Figure 80c**).

Figure 80c An expanded list of the styles in a menu bar.

Every menu bar generates at least a dozen CSS styles. Selecting one of these Class styles in the top part of the CSS Styles panel allows you to edit properties for that style in the bottom half of the CSS Styles panel.

To change the background or text color for the menu bar, select the style ul.MenuBarHorizontal a (or for a vertical menu bar, select the style ul.MenuBarVertical a). With the style selected in the CSS Styles panel, use the background color swatch box in the bottom half of the CSS Styles panel to choose a new background color and use the Color swatch to change font color.

Change the background and text color of a hovered over horizontal menu option using the (awkwardly named) ul.MenuBarHorizontal a.MenuBarItemHover, ul.MenuBarHorizontal a.MenuBarItemSubmenuH over, ul.MenuBarHorizontal a.MenuBarSubmenuVisible menu. The style for vertical menu bars is similar, but Vertical is used in place of Horizontal in the style name.

When you save the page in which the Spry menu bar is embedded, the style sheet file associated with the menu bar updates.

Test your Spry menu bar in Live view (**Figure 80d**).

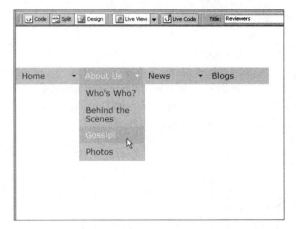

Figure 80d Testing a Spry menu bar in Live view.

#81 Inserting Tabbed Panels

Deleting Tabbed Panels

You can delete a tabbed panel by selecting it in the Property inspector and clicking the "–" icon in the Panels area. Also, you can move a selected tabbed panel up or down in the Property inspector using the Up and Down triangles in the Panels area. Moving a selected panel up moves that panel to the left in the tabbed panel order.

Tabbed panels transform a single Web page into a series of tabbed panels that look like distinct Web pages to a visitor. Tabbed panels are one way to create an easily navigable Web site.

To create a set of tabbed panels for an open Web page, choose Insert > Spry > Tabbed Panels. A generic set of two tabbed panels appears in the Document window.

To change the title of a tab, click on the tab and enter a new name for the tab. To enter content in a tabbed panel, click a tab. The selected tab displays a blue outline. Click in the Content area below the tab and enter content for that tab. Tab content can be anything you would place on a regular Web page, including text and images (**Figure 81a**).

Figure 81a Entering content into a tabbed panel.

You can add (or delete) tabbed panels for a selected tabbed panel in the Property inspector. To select an *entire tabbed panel* as opposed to a single tab, click the border of the entire tabbed panel. When you do this, the Tabbed Panels Property inspector allows you to add panels by clicking the "+" icon in the Panels section of the Property inspector (**Figure 81b**).

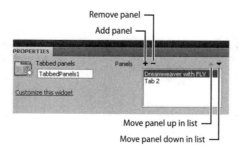

Figure 81b Adding a tabbed panel in the Property inspector.

Chances are you will not want your tabbed panels named Tab 1, Tab 2, and so on. Instead, you'll want tab names that reflect the content of the actual tab, like "Home," "Contact Info," "About Us," or whatever label makes sense for your content. To change the name of a tabbed panel, double-click the current label (for example, Tab 1) and type a new label.

Tip

When you hover over a tabbed panel, you will see an eye icon. Clicking the eye icon makes the tabbed panel invisible. This is a technique that can be used with JavaScript to make tabs appear and disappear. That level of JavaScripting is beyond the scope of this book, but be aware that if you do click the eye icon, the selected tab will not be visible.

To format elements of the tab like background and text color, select the CSS Styles panel (choose Window > CSS Styles) and view the styles for the SpryTabbedPanels.css. When you expand this CSS file in the CSS Styles panel, a set of Class styles appears in the CSS Styles panel. In the lower part of the CSS Styles panel, you can change the properties of any style you select in the top part of the panel. The sidebar, "Use the CSS Styles Panel to Format Tabbed Panels," explains how to edit frequently changed elements of a panel style. Feel free to experiment with other properties.

For example, to change background color for nonselected tabs, click the .Tabbed PanelsTab style in the CSS Styles panel, and then choose a background color from the background-color property (**Figure 81c**).

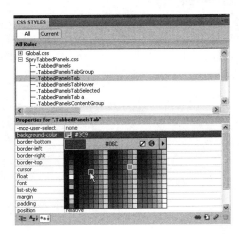

Figure 81c Changing the background color for nonselected tabs.

Use the CSS Styles Panel to Format Tabbed Panels

You can change the background color of tabbed panel elements in the CSS Styles panel:

- To change the background color for a hovered-over tab, choose the .Tabbed PanelsTabHover style in the CSS Styles panel, and then choose a background color from the background-color property.

- To change the background color for a selected tab, choose the .TabbedPanels TabSelected style in the CSS Styles panel, and then choose a background color from the background-color property.

- To change the background color for a tabbed content area, select that tab in the Document window, choose the .Tabbed PanelsContentGroup style in the CSS Styles panel, and then choose a background color from the background-color property.

Format the content of tabbed panels the same way you format text or images.

#82 Inserting a Spry Accordion Widget

View the styles associated with the Spry accordion in the CSS Styles panel. The CSS file with the styles for the Accordion widget is SprY Accordion.css. Select and expand that style in the CSS Styles panel to see the class styles associated with your accordion panel.

- To format the tab background color for non-selected tabs, edit the background-color property in the .Accordion-Panel Tab style. For the selected tab, edit the .AccordionPanel Open .Accordion PanelTab style.

- To change the text color that displays when a user hovers over a tab for an unopened accordion panel, edit the color property of the .AccordionPanel TabHover style. For an opened accordion panel, edit the .AccordionPanelOpen .AccordionPanel TabHover style.

The Spry Accordion widget creates horizontal regions on a Web page that can be expanded or collapsed. Only one of these regions can be expanded at any one time. Accordion regions have the benefit of allowing visitors to your site to view or hide some but not all of your page content, reducing clutter and allowing them to focus on the content they want to see.

To insert a Spry accordion, first save your page, and then choose Insert > Spry > Spry Accordion. By default, a two-part accordion is created with Label 1 and Content 1 on top, and Label 2 and Content 2 on the bottom. In the Document window, click and drag to select the default text, "Label 1," and enter a new label for the accordion section—this is what users will see in their browser window and what they will click to expand that accordion section. In the Content 1 area, delete the "Content 1" default text and enter new page content. That page content can be anything you would put on a regular Web page—images, text, media, and so on. Customize the second Spry accordion section in the same way.

You can add or delete Spry accordion sections for a selected accordion in the Property inspector. Use the Add Panel or Remove Panel icon to add panels or to delete a selected panel. Use the Move Panel Up List and Move Panel Down List icons to rearrange the order of your panels (**Figure 82**).

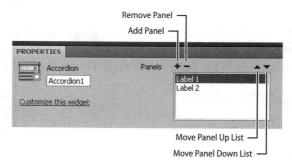

Figure 82 The Spry Accordion Property inspector.

#83 Inserting a Spry Collapsible Panel Widget

Spry collapsible panels are handy ways to present optional information in a Web page. Spry collapsible panels have a clickable tab and a content area that displays or hides when a visitor clicks the tab.

The Web page that I use to check my bank balance, for example, has a number of clickable spots on the page where I can get explanations for terms or see additional detail. This information might not be necessary for a visitor and would in many cases clutter the page. But when presented in a collapsible panel, such information is handy but doesn't take up space.

To insert a Spry collapsible panel, first save your page, and then choose Insert > Spry > Spry Collapsible Panel. In the Document window, click and drag to select the default text, "tab," and enter a new label for the collapsible panel. Visitors will see this label in their browser window. Clicking this tab label in a browser toggles between displaying and hiding the panel. In the Content area of the collapsible panel, delete the "Content" default text and enter new page content. That page content can be anything you would put on a regular Web page (**Figure 83**).

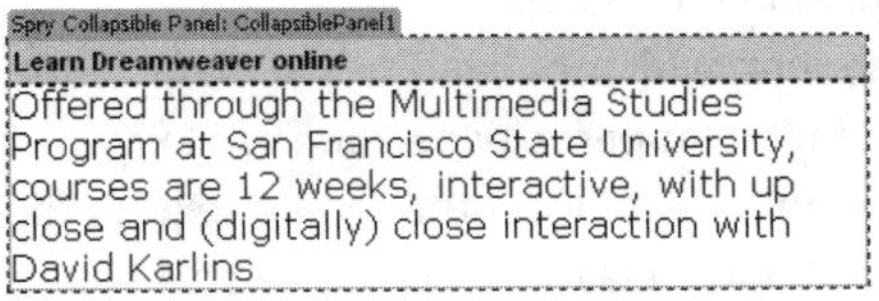

Spry Collapsible Panel: CollapsiblePanel1

Learn Dreamweaver online
Offered through the Multimedia Studies Program at San Francisco State University, courses are 12 weeks, interactive, with up close and (digitally) close interaction with David Karlins

Figure 83 Entering tab and expandable text for a Spry collapsible panel.

Like other Spry widgets, you can edit basic features of the Collapsible Panel widget in the Property inspector (see the sidebar, "Hide or Display Spry Collapsible Panels?"). To format elements of the widget like background and text color, select the CSS Styles panel (choose Window > CSS Styles) and view the styles for the SpryCollapsiblePanel.css sheet by expanding that style sheet.

The main property of a collapsible panel that you will need to edit in the CSS Styles panel is the background color for the tab. You can edit the actual tab text in the Property inspector. But to edit the background of the collapsible panel tab, edit the background-color property of the .CollapsiblePanelTab style.

Hide or Display Spry Collapsible Panels?

When you create or select a Spry collapsible panel, the Property inspector has two menus: Display and Default State. If you choose Open from the Display menu, the collapsible panel is always open in the Document window. Independently of that, you can choose either Open or Closed from the Default State menu. If you choose Open, which is the default, the Spry collapsible panel is open when a visitor opens your Web page and only collapses if he or she clicks the tab. In my opinion, this basically defeats the purpose of a collapsible panel, and most of the time you will want to choose Closed from the Default State menu.

#84 Define a Spry Tooltip

Spry tooltips generate tooltip content for specific text. To create a Spry tooltip, click to place your cursor at an insertion point where the tooltip text will appear (don't type the tooltip trigger text first; creating the trigger text is part of the Tooltip properties that you define later).

With your insertion point where the trigger text for the tooltip will appear, choose Insert > Spry > Spry Tooltip. Two items appear in your document: text that displays as "Tooltip trigger goes here" and a box with default text displaying "Tooltip content goes here" (**Figure 84**).

Tooltip trigger goes here.
Tooltip content goes here.

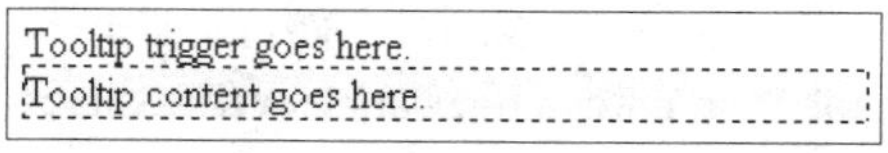

Figure 84 Default text for tooltip trigger and tooltip content.

Replace the text "Tooltip trigger goes here" with the text that you want to trigger the tooltip. Replace the text that says "Tooltip content goes here" with the text that will appear in the tooltip.

Tooltip properties usually are fine without changing the default settings, but they can be adjusted in the Property inspector. The Horizontal and Vertical Offset boxes define how far to offset the tooltip text (to the right and down respectively). The Show Delay and Hide Delay boxes allow you to enter values (in seconds) for how long to wait to display tooltip text after the trigger text is hovered over and how long to wait after the trigger text is no longer hovered over to hide the tooltip.

The Blind and Fade options generate effects that are not appropriate for displaying useful, readable tooltip text, and the Hide on Mouse Out check box is not operative. The Follow mouse check box moves tooltip text as a user's mouse moves within the trigger text.

CHAPTER FOURTEEN

Using Spry Data Sets

The ability to add data (including images) to a table and have that data instantly reflected in a Web page opens up tremendous potential for maintaining a fresh, frequently updated Web site.

Dreamweaver CS4 introduces important new techniques for creating and updating data tables, and reflecting that data in a variety of attractive Web pages: Spry Data Sets.

There are two basic steps to setting up and using Spry Data Sets:

1. Create a data table that will serve as the Spry Data Source.

2. Create a Spry Data Display in a separate Web page to display that data.

Once you have the Spry Data Source table and the Spry Data Display page set up, you can easily update the data, and that new content will instantly display in the Spry Data Display.

#85 Creating a Spry Data Source Table

The easiest and most accessible way to create a Spry Data Source is to define and populate a table that lists all the information you want to display in the Spry Data Display. The Spry Data Display you generate on a separate Web page will be attractive and accessible. The Spry Data Display table does not have to be attractive because it will only be seen and used by whoever updates it.

Note

In this how-to, I focus on the steps required to build a table to store data for a Spry Data Source. For a fuller discussion of how to create and format tables and table cells, see #20, "Creating a Table," #23, "Defining Table Properties," and #24, "Formatting Cells."

Data tables are generally organized into *columns* that reflect *fields* and *rows* that reflect specific items (referred to as "records" in database terminology). So, for example, a product database might include *fields* like Product, Product Code, Price, Description, and Image (the last being a photo of the product). In such a table, each *row* would hold information for a specific product (**Figure 85a**).

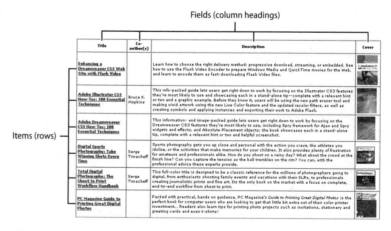

Figure 85a A Spry Data Source table populated with fields and items.

To create a Spry Data Source table, follow these steps:

1. Create a new HTML page (choose File > New to open the New Document dialog, choose Blank Page from the category list on the left, choose HTML / None as the page type, and click Create).

2. Save the page (assign a filename like "data01" to help you remember that this is the page that holds your Spry Data Source table.

3. Choose Insert > Table to open the Table dialog. In the Columns box, enter the number of *fields* (columns) required to organize your data.

4. Leave the Rows box set to the default number. You can easily add rows to your table as you enter new items into it.

5. Leave the Border set to 1.

6. Set Table Width to 100% to create the most convenient layout to enter data.

7. Set Cell Padding to 6 to make the table data more readable (cell padding provides a buffer between the different rows and columns of data).

8. In the Header area of the dialog, select Top. This provides automatic formatting for your column headings.

9. You can enter a caption to improve accessibility if the table will be used by people with visual handicaps.

10. After you complete the Table dialog (**Figure 85b**), click OK to generate the table.

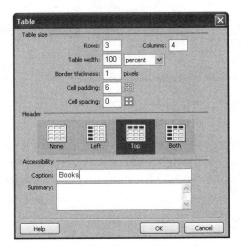

Figure 85b Defining a table to use as a Spry Data Source.

(*continued on next page*)

11. With the table generated, enter column headings (field names) in the top row of the table (**Figure 85c**).

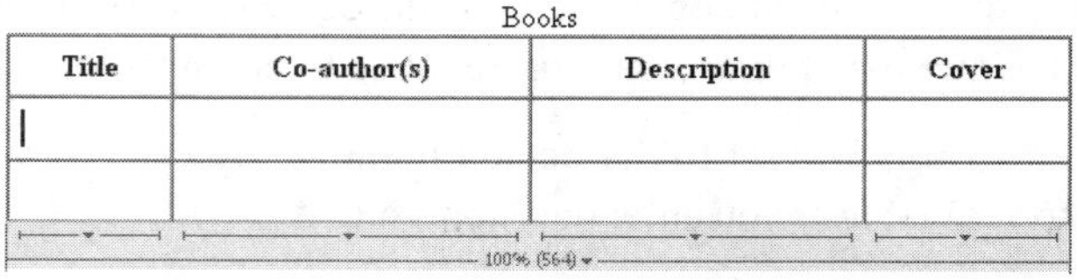

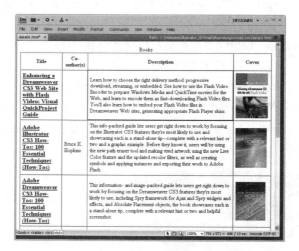

Figure 85c A Spry Data Source table with field names.

12. Populate the Spry Data Source table with information for your database. Use a separate row for each item (**Figure 85d**).

Figure 85d Entering data in a Spry Data Source table.

13. The last and important step in creating a Spry Data Source table is to name the table using the Table box in the Property inspector. To do this, select the table by clicking on the table border. In the Table box, enter a name for your table. Avoid spaces or nonalphanumeric characters.

#86 Generating a Spry Data Display

You can insert a Spry Data Display in any existing Web page, or you can create a new Web page and use the entire page to display the Spry Data Display. The only trick is that you must have first created a Spry Data Source (if you haven't done that, jump back to #85, "Creating a Spry Data Source Table").

To generate the Spry Data Display, follow these steps:

1. Choose Insert > Spry > Spry Data Set. The Spry Data Set wizard launches.

2. In the Select Data Type pop-up menu, choose HTML.

3. Click the Browse button in the Specify Data File area and navigate to and select the file you created with the Spry Data Source table. Your data table displays in the preview area.

4. From the Data Containers pop-up menu, choose the specific table with your data (**Figure 86a**).

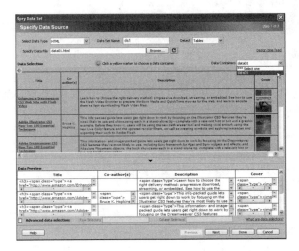

Figure 86a Choosing a data table to embed as a Spry Data Display.

5. With the data source defined, click the Next button in the Spry Data Set wizard. Normally, there is no reason to change the default options in step 2 of the wizard. However, if you are comfortable with database management concepts, you can use the Type pop-up menu to change

(continued on next page)

the way data is recognized (for example, if you are sorting dates in 12/12/09 format), and you can sort rows. After examining the settings in step 2, click Next.

6. The final step in the Spry Data Set wizard allows you to choose from four different layouts to display your data. Each layout option includes a thumbnail illustration and a description. Choose one of the layout options. (The fifth option, Do Not Insert HTML, voids the whole point of the wizard and is for programmers who want to define custom data presentation).

7. With a layout selected, click the Set Up button associated with your choice. Each layout includes customized and different Set Up options, but they all boil down to the ability to add, delete, or change the order of display of columns. Use the Add, Delete, Up, or Down arrows to adjust the displays (**Figure 86b**).

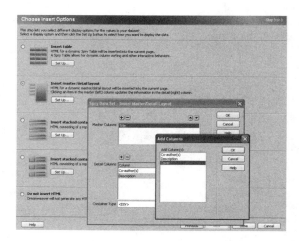

Figure 86b Adding a column (Cover) to the Master Column display in the Master/Detail Layout.

8. After adjusting layout options, if desired, click Done in the Spry Data Set wizard to generate the Spry Data Set layout.

You can preview the Spry Data Display in Live view (choose View > Live View).

#**87** Testing and Updating a Spry Data Source or Display

You can test your Spry Data Display by viewing the Web page with the display in Live view (choose View > Live View to toggle between Live view and Edit view). Or, you can preview the Web page with your Spry Data Display in a browser. To do that, choose File > Preview in Browser and select an installed browser (**Figure 87a**).

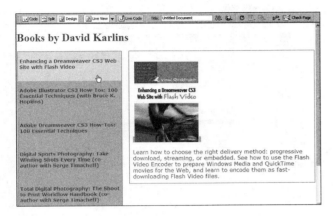

Figure 87a Previewing a Spry Data Display.

It's easy to update the data in a Spry Data Source. When you open the Web page with your Spry Data Source table, you can simply add, edit, or delete data. As you save the page with the Spry Data Source table, the data displayed in the Spry Data Display (on a separate Web page) updates automatically.

Changing the layout of the Spry Data Display is not as simple. There is no nice, easy way to reopen the Spry Data Set wizard and change display settings.

If you want to substantially revise your Spry Data Display layout, the best way to do that is to delete your existing layout and go through the wizard again!

That said, for the brave and adventurous, or if you just want to slightly tweak or customize a generated Spry Data Display layout, you can select any CSS object generated as part of a Spry Data Display and experiment with customizing or editing the features of that object in the CSS Styles panel. Refer to #33, "Editing Layout Div Tags in the CSS Styles Panel,"

Why Isn't There an Easier Way to Revise a Spry Data Display?

Spry Data Displays involve a large number of generated CSS objects for page layout. And those CSS objects are very different for each of the four layouts (and layout options make the differences even more complex). Given all that, it doesn't take that long and is pretty simple to redefine a *new* Spry Data Display if you want to change your data display layout.

and #38, "Create Class CSS Formatting Rules for Text," as you experiment with customizing the CSS objects generated by the Spry Data Display (**Figure 87b**).

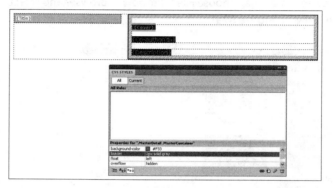

Figure 87b Tinkering with the generated CSS format in a Spry Data Display.

CHAPTER FIFTEEN

Adding Interactivity with Behaviors

Dreamweaver behaviors generate JavaScript and CSS to provide tools like browser detection scripts, pop-up messages, and effects. With CS4, Adobe continues the process of evolving away from behaviors, which were inherited from previous versions of Dreamweaver. Instead, Spry widgets provide many features, like form validation scripts, that used to be handled by behaviors (see Chapter 11, "Defining Spry Validation Widgets" for form validation techniques in Dreamweaver CS4).

That said, Dreamweaver behaviors continue to be supported and still provide the best way to open a new browser window, create a pop-up box, or apply effects like shrink or fade.

Dreamweaver generates behaviors using the Behaviors panel. In the Behaviors panel, you define two elements to every action: events and actions. *Events* trigger *actions*. An event might be a page opening or closing, or a visitor hovering a mouse cursor over an object on the page. An action is generated by an event. Examples of actions include an image changing, a pop-up window opening, or a sound going off.

Many behaviors are defined interactively in the Behaviors panel—you choose from a list of possible events, and then choose an associated action. Other animated and interactive elements in Dreamweaver can be generated from the main menu in the Document window.

#88 Choosing Browser Support for Behaviors

JavaScript is interpreted by browsers, but some browsers don't support all Dreamweaver-generated JavaScript. For this reason, the first step in defining most behaviors is to identify the browsing environment you are designing for. Browsers like Safari, Firefox, and Internet Explorer have built-in support for JavaScript. Older browsers and older versions of Internet Explorer do not support as much JavaScript as newer browsers.

By default, Dreamweaver displays only behaviors that work in nearly all browsers. If you accept this default setting, your set of available behaviors is quite restricted. And, in most cases, unnecessarily so. Very few Web surfers are still cruising the Web with Netscape Navigator 4.0.

To change the default set of available behaviors, click the "+" button in the Behaviors panel. Choose Show Events For from the pop-up menu, and then select one of the available browsers and browser versions (**Figure 88**).

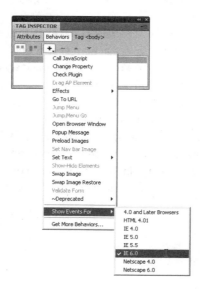

Figure 88 Choosing a browser and version for available Dreamweaver behaviors.

Dreamweaver's set of available browsers remains sadly out of date. However, Internet Explorer 6 is a de facto standard that most other browsers adhere to, so behaviors that work in Internet Explorer 6 are likely to work in other browsers.

#**89** Opening a Browser Window

They're often called pop-ups—those little browser windows that open when you load a page in your browser or when you activate the window by some action on the Web page. In Dreamweaver's terminology, they are referred to as *browser windows*, which is actually an accurate description of what most people call pop-ups.

The first step in creating a behavior that will open a browser window is to create a special Web page that will appear in that browser window. Since this page is likely to be displayed in a small browser window (you will be defining the size of that browser window as part of the behavior), you should design a page that will work well in a small browser window (**Figure 89a**).

Open Browser Window Triggers

By default, the open browser window behavior uses the page loading as the triggering event. In other words, the new browser window opens as soon as a visitor opens the launching page in his or her browser.

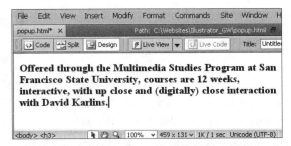

Figure 89a Defining a Web page with a very small amount of content to use as a new pop-up browser window.

With the Web page that will open in a new browser window prepared and saved, follow these steps to define the window:

1. From the Behaviors panel, click the "+" button and choose Open Browser Window from the list of behaviors.

2. In the URL to display field, navigate to or enter the Web page that will open in the new browser window.

(continued on next page)

3. Use the Window width and Window height fields to define the size of the browser window (**Figure 89b**).

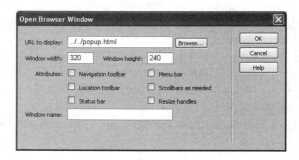

Figure 89b Defining height and width for the pop-up browser window.

4. The display options available in the Attributes section of the Open Browser Window dialog are generally *not* enabled—the new browser window that pops up is usually displayed without features like a navigation toolbar or status bar. So, leave these options deselected.

5. Enter a name in the Window name field, and then click OK in the Open Browser Window dialog.

Test your new browser window behavior by opening the page that launches it in a browser.

You can change the triggering event that opens a new browser window. For example, you can have a visitor click specific text to open the new browser window. To do this, follow these steps:

1. In the Behaviors panel, click the Open Browser Window behavior in the list. Click the "–" icon to delete this behavior. You will define a new behavior that will launch the new browser window using a different event.

2. Enter text on your page that will serve as a link to open the new browser window. In the Property inspector, enter the pound symbol (#) in the Link field to create a self-referring link. This will display the text as a link, even though the result of clicking the link will be defined by a behavior.

3. With the text you defined as a self-referring link in step 2 selected, define an Open Browser Window behavior just as you did in steps 1–5 earlier in this technique. However, this time—because you had link text selected—the default triggering event is not onLoad (when the page opens) but onClick (when the selected text is clicked).

If onClick is not set as the triggering event, you can select it from the first column pop-up menu in the Behaviors panel (**Figure 89c**).

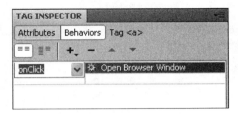

Figure 89c Defining onClick as the trigger to open a new browser window.

Or, if you want to use a different triggering event (such as onMouseOver—when a visitor hovers a mouse cursor over the selected text), you can choose a different event from the first column pop-up menu in the Behaviors panel.

#90 Designing a Pop-up Message

Triggering a Pop-up Message

If you want a pop-up message to be triggered by clicking (or applying some other action to) text or an image, select the text or image. Then, pick up at step 2 in the instructions on this page to define the pop-up content and triggering action.

Pop-up messages present dialogs with information and require a visitor to OK them before they will close.

To create a pop-up message that displays a dialog, follow these steps:

1. If you want the pop-up (new browser window) to appear when the page loads, click the <body> tag in the Tag Selector bar on the bottom of the Document window (**Figure 90a**).

Figure 90a The Body tag in the status bar of the Dreamweaver Document window.

2. In the Behaviors panel, click the "+" button to activate the list of available behaviors, and choose Popup Message.

3. In the Popup Message dialog, enter the message visitors will see when the pop-up message is triggered, and then click OK (**Figure 90b**).

Figure 90b Entering a pop-up message.

4. Test the pop-up message by previewing the page in a browser.

5. If you want the pop-up message to be triggered by clicking (or performing another action on) link text or an image, select that image before generating the pop-up behavior. If it is often difficult to tell which object you have selected, you can select the object in the Tag Selector bar or verify that the object is selected in the Tag Selector bar. Choose a triggering event like onClick from the Events column in the Behaviors panel.

#91 Applying Effects

Effects like blinds, fades, or highlighting can be applied to almost any element on a Web page, including an image or a link.

Effects include the following:

- Appear/Fade makes the selected object appear or fade away.

- Blind creates a window blind-like effect that hides and reveals the object.

- Grow/Shrink makes the object bigger or smaller.

- Highlight changes the background color of the object.

- Shake moves the object from left to right.

- Slide moves the object up or down.

- Squish makes the object vanish into the upper-left corner of the page.

To apply an effect to a selected object, choose Effect from the Behaviors panel menu, and then choose one of the available effects (**Figure 91**).

Effect Settings

Each Dreamweaver effect has settings parameters. Some are pretty self-explanatory, like effect duration (determines how long the effect lasts). Others are hard to explain. In reality, you'll experiment with various settings to see how the effect works in a browser.

Figure 91 Selecting an effect.

Each effect has its own dialog with its own features.

#92 Deleting Behaviors

Deleting behaviors can be confusing and frustrating. This is one of the tasks my students most often call me over to their workstations to help them with. So, let me demystify that process.

Deleting a behavior involves two steps—finding the behavior in the Behaviors panel, and then deleting it. The first step is the hard part. The trick to locating a behavior in the Behaviors panel is to first select the object to which the behavior is associated. Only then will the behavior be easy to find in the Behaviors panel. Once you select the behavior in the Behaviors panel, click the "–" (Remove Event) icon to delete the behavior (**Figure 92**).

Remove Event icon

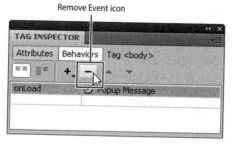

Figure 92 Removing a behavior in the Behaviors panel.

What about events that are *not* attached to any object on a page but instead are attached to the actual page? These behaviors can be the hardest to find. But you can see them in the Behaviors panel if you click the <body> tag in the Tag Selector bar at the bottom of the Document window. Events that launch when a page is loaded or exited will likely be associated with the <body> tag.

CHAPTER SIXTEEN

Testing and Maintaining Sites

Basic site maintenance like checking and fixing broken links, cleaning up bad HTML imported with text from Microsoft Word, and checking browser compatibility and accessibility makes the difference between professional Web pages and carelessly maintained Web sites.

Dreamweaver provides a robust set of tools for making sure your site is error free and ensuring that visitors' experience at your site is not marred with busted links.

This chapter explores the most useful of those tools.

#93 Defining Check Page Settings

Buried in the Dreamweaver Document toolbar is a useful icon that controls how Dreamweaver checks your Web pages to ensure compatibility with browsers. This icon also opens menus that produce reports on browser compatibility issues.

Dreamweaver can check your page to make sure it is compatible with any combination of Firefox, Internet Explorer for Windows, Internet Explorer for Mac, Mozilla, Netscape Navigator, Opera, and Safari. Several versions of each of these browsers are supported by this feature.

To define the browsers with which Dreamweaver will check your page for compatibility, click the Check Page icon in the Document toolbar and choose Settings (**Figure 93a**).

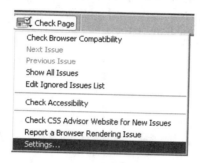

Figure 93a Accessing browser check settings in the Document toolbar.

Tip

If the Document toolbar is not visible, choose View > Toolbars > Document to display it.

The Settings selection opens the Target Browsers dialog. Here you define which browsers and which version of each selected browser will be used to test your page. Choose browsers by selecting the check box next to the browser and choosing a version of that browser from the accompanying pop-up menu (**Figure 93b**).

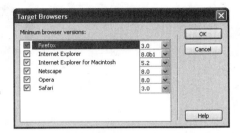

Figure 93b Defining the set of browsers for which Dreamweaver will test your page for compatibility.

After you OK the Target Browsers dialog, your pages will be tested for browser compatibility issues with the set of browsers you defined.

#94 Checking Browser Compatibility

You can check pages for browser compatibility issues by choosing Check Browser Compatibility from the Check Page menu in the Document toolbar (**Figure 94**).

Figure 94 Viewing a list of browser compatibility issues for a page.

Or, you can view a list of all browser compatibility issues in any open document by choosing Show All Issues from the menu. When you do this, a list of errors appears telling you which features are not supported in different browsers.

The list of browser compatibility issues that appears in the Browser Compatibility Check window requires some familiarity with coding or the ability to decipher coding to interpret the issues. The Issue column describes the support issue, and the Line column identifies the line of coding in Code view. If you know some HTML, you might be able to tweak the code. Or even if you don't, you can often figure out what the problem is and delete the element in your Web page (a CSS style, for example) that shows up on the list of issues.

#95 Previewing Web Pages in Device Central

Are you curious as to how your Web page will look when viewed on various models of cell phones? When you preview Web pages in Adobe Device Central CS4, you can see how your Web page will look on a wide range of viewing devices.

To preview an open page in Device Central, choose File > Preview in Browser > Device Central. Device Central opens in a new window. From the list of devices on the left side of the window, click an expand arrow to see a list of all versions of the mobile phone or other device. For example, if you want to see how your page will look on a device that supports Flash Lite 1.1, select that standard from the Device Sets list (**Figure 95**).

Figure 95 Previewing a Web page as it will appear in Flash Lite 1.1.

You will see that the list of devices in Device Central also indicates the display size of the viewing area on that device. This information is listed right next to the device model.

Not only can you preview your open Web page in Device Central, but once you open the page, you can also navigate around your Web site (or around the Web if you need to for some reason) right in the preview environment device you selected.

Need to Design for a Device Not in Device Central?

If you are designing for a device that is not available in Device Central or if you are designing for a mobile browsing environment and don't know which device you are designing for, you can simply find a device that has dimensions that match your parameters. For example, if you are designing a Web page that needs to be viewed on a screen with dimensions of 240 pixels by 320 pixels, you can preview that page in any of the many devices that have screens that size.

#96 Testing Links Sitewide

The dreaded "404 (page not found)" error is not an experience you want visitors to your Web site to have. When visitors follow links on your site to pages that don't work—either on or outside your site—an error message appears in their browser and, of course, they do not see the page that the link was supposed to open. Dreamweaver can easily and quickly test all the links in your site, both internal (links to files on your site) and external (links to pages and other files outside your site). Dreamweaver can also identify *orphan* pages—pages to which there is no link.

To test all links and identify orphan pages, follow these steps:

1. With or without a page open in the Document window, choose Site > Check Links Sitewide.

2. You can choose from the three reports in the Show pop-up menu in the Report window that opens after you check links. The Broken Links view shows bad links within your site. The External Links view lists links to Web sites or pages outside your site that are no longer good. The Orphaned Files view displays files to which there is no link from any page in your site (**Figure 96**).

Figure 96 Viewing broken links to files outside your site.

3. You can fix a broken link by double-clicking a link in the list of either the Broken Links or the External Links reports. The page with the bad link will open, and the link will be highlighted. You can delete or edit the URL for the bad link in the Document window just as you would normally edit a page.

#97 Testing Accessibility

Accessibility means the ability of people with various types of disabilities to access a Web site. How you apply accessibility depends on your audience and the purpose of your site. There are formal standards and legal issues, as well as informal communities that promote Web accessible design techniques.

In the United States, Section 508 of the Federal Rehabilitation Act requires access to electronic and information technology procured by Federal agencies. You can review those standards at www.access-board.gov/508.htm.

The Web Accessibility Initiative (WCAG) promotes techniques and standards for Web accessibility. The WCAG Web site is at www.w3.org/WAI.

Dreamweaver CS4 will test your site and identify accessibility issues. To check the accessibility of your site, choose Check Accessibility from the Check Page menu in the Document toolbar (**Figure 97a**).

Figure 97a Checking accessibility.

A list appears that identifies accessibility issues. The elements identified in the list are not very self-explanatory. You can, however, get more information on identified issues by looking up those identified issues at the WCAG Web site. Dreamweaver's Accessibility Issues report identifies the WCAG Guideline associated with the accessibility issues that it lists (**Figure 97b**).

Associated WCAG Guideline

File	Line	Description
? TTip.html	7	Objects should not cause movement [WCAG 7.3 P2] -- MANUAL -- SCRIPT i...
? TTip.html	23	Objects should have device-independent interface [WCAG 9.2 P2] -- MANU...
? TTip.html	24	Objects should have device-independent interface [WCAG 9.2 P2] -- MANU...
? TTip.html	2	Use last appropriate W3C technologies [WCAG 11.1 P2] -- MANUAL --
? TTip.html	2	Divide information into appropriate manageable groups [WCAG 12.3 P2] -- ...
× TTip.html	2	Provide metadata to pages and sites [WCAG 13.2 P2] -- FAILED --
? TTip.html	2	Provide information about site organization [WCAG 13.3 P2] -- MANUAL --

Figure 97b Accessibility issues report.

Accessibility Tips

Many sites and organizations provide tips for accessible page design. Useit.com (www.useit.com) has served for many years as a comprehensive resource for, and a model of, applying Web accessibility techniques.

#98 Cleaning Up Word HTML

Getting Word Documents into Dreamweaver

There are a number of ways to convert Word text to HTML. You can choose to save a Word file as HTML, and then open that HTML file in Dreamweaver and edit it, or you can copy and paste text from Word into a Dreamweaver document. If you choose File > Paste Special, the Paste Special dialog provides a number of options for how to handle Word formatting when text is copied from Word to Dreamweaver.

Frequently, text used in your Web pages is created in Microsoft Word. Depending on the options you choose when importing Word text into Dreamweaver, the HTML that is generated will range from slightly flawed to really weird. If you elect to preserve all formatting from Word documents (which happens if you save a Word document as an HTML page and open it in Dreamweaver), the HTML code is full of proprietary Microsoft codes that make the page confusing to edit and format.

To clean up HTML pages with imported Word text, choose Commands > Cleanup Word HTML. The Clean Up Word HTML dialog opens (**Figure 98a**).

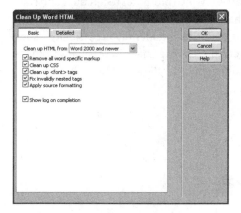

Figure 98a Cleaning up Word HTML.

Normally, you can accept the defaults in this dialog (all options are selected) and click OK. If you are using a pre–Word 2000 version of Microsoft Word, choose that version from the Clean up HTML from pop-up menu.

After you click OK in the Clean Up Word HTML dialog, another dialog opens telling you what Word HTML was fixed in the process (**Figure 98b**).

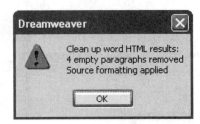

Figure 98b Results of cleaning up Word HTML.

If you are curious as to what kind of nonstandard HTML is fixed by the clean up Word HTML process or if you are an HTML and CSS coder and want to manage this process in detail, click the Detailed tab in the Clean Up Word HTML dialog. You can observe or change the fixes applied to Word HTML.

Copying Word Text and Preserving Formatting

The Paste Special dialog box that is available when you paste Word text into a Dreamweaver document provides a few levels of preserving formatting, ranging from preserving very little formatting from the Word document to preserving almost all.

If you choose the Text only option in the Paste Special dialog, only text is pasted. This option allows you to reformat text in Dreamweaver without worrying about formatting imported from Word. Choosing the text with structure plus full formatting (bold, italic, styles) option imports not only all formatting, but also style definitions (like Heading 1) that are converted in Dreamweaver to CSS styles.

#99 Adding Design Notes

If you are working on a Web site with others or simply want to add Post-it-type notes to pages to remind you of items to fix, you can attach Design Notes to pages. Design Notes can be configured to open when a page is opened in Dreamweaver.

To add a Design Note to an open page, choose File > Design Notes. The Design Notes dialog opens (**Figure 99**). Here you can define a status from the Status pop-up menu. There are eight available status settings, including draft, final, and needs attention.

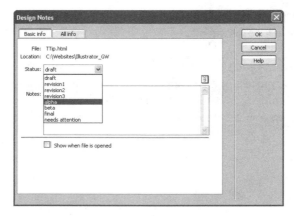

Figure 99 Status options for a Design Note.

In the Notes area, enter any text you desire. Select the Show when file is opened check box to have the notes appear when you open a page for editing in Dreamweaver. These notes never appear in a browser.

#100 Testing Browsers for Media Support

Media files require plug-in software to be played in a browser. A large percentage of folks who browse the Web have downloaded and installed players for Windows Media, QuickTime, and Flash files.

On the other hand, not everyone has downloaded players that support all the main media file types. Dreamweaver generates a quick, easy behavior that will detect browsers that do not have a defined media player installed, and then reroute these visitors to an alternate page in your site that does not require that particular plug-in to make the page work.

The behavior that tests a visitor's browser for plug-in support is triggered by a page loading in a browser window. To facilitate this happening correctly, select the <body> tag in the tag selection area on the left side of the status bar in the Document window generating the behavior.

Follow these steps to generate a behavior that will test browsers for plug-in support for a media player:

1. With the <body> tag selected in the open page's tag selection area, click the "+" button in the Behaviors panel and choose Check Plugin. The Check Plugin dialog opens (**Figure 100a**).

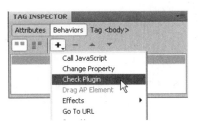

Figure 100a Opening the Check Plugin dialog.

2. With the Select radio button selected, choose one of the available media types from the pop-up menu (**Figure 100b**).

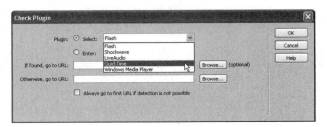

Figure 100b Choosing a plug-in to test for when the page is opened.

(continued on next page)

Why Select the Body Tag First?

By selecting the <body> tag before defining a behavior, you are allowing an action that affects the entire Web page (like loading the page in a browser) to be the triggering action for that behavior. See a more developed discussion of how Dreamweaver uses behaviors to generate JavaScript and other interactive and dynamic script and code in Chapter 15, "Adding Interactivity with Behaviors."

244

Other Plug-ins?

For all practical purposes, the plug-ins you can test for with a generated behavior are constrained to the list in the Select pop-up menu. Theoretically, you could enter the name of another plug-in in the Enter field, but this option requires knowing exactly how to formulate the name of a plug-in in a way that generated JavaScript can manage it.

3. The If found, go to URL field is optional and typically not used. If the page to which you are applying the behavior is the page with the media that requires a plug-in, visitors who do have that plug-in will stay on this page by default.

4. In the Otherwise, go to URL field, enter the (full) URL of the alternate page that contains a version of the page content that does not require the selected plug-in. If the alternate page is a file in your Web site, you can navigate to and select that file with the Browse button.

5. Selecting the Always Go to first URL if detection is not possible check box opens the current page if the script is not able to determine whether the plug-in is installed. Sometimes visitors have Flash or another plug-in installed, but the testing script is unable to determine this. If you select this check box, visitors will be diverted to the alternate page only if the testing script definitively determines that they do *not* have plug-in support for the selected media type. After you define the whole behavior, click OK.

Index